At Sylvan, we believe reading is one of life's most important, most personal, most meaningful skills, and we're so glad you've taken this step to become a successful reader with us. We know spelling is a critical process that mirrors and complements the reading process. Fourth-grade spellers are learning to spell more words with prefixes and suffixes, as well as roots. A strong foundation in spelling prepares fourth-graders to spell more challenging words in upcoming grades and makes them stronger readers.

At Sylvan, successful spelling instruction encompasses numerous spelling processes with research-based, developmentally appropriate, and highly motivating, entertaining, and thought-provoking lessons. The learning process relies on high standards and meaningful parental involvement. With success, students feel increasing confidence. With increasing confidence, students build even more success. It's a perfect cycle. That's why our Sylvan workbooks aren't like the others. We're laying out the roadmap for learning. The rest is in your hands.

Parents, you have a special role. While your child is working, stay within earshot. If he needs help or gets stuck, you can be there to get him on the right track. And you're always there with supportive encouragement and plenty of celebratory congratulations.

One of the best ways to master spelling is to check one's own work. Often the answer is just a dictionary away, so that's always a good place to start. Each section of the workbook also includes a Check It! strip. As your child completes the activities, he can check his answers with Check It! If he sees any errors, he can fix them himself.

At Sylvan, our goal is confident spellers who have the skills to tackle anything they want to read. We love learning. We want all children to love it as well.

Included with your purchase is a coupon for a discount on our in-center service. As your child continues on his academic journey, your local Sylvan Learning Center can partner with your family in ensuring your child remains a confident, successful, and independent learner.

The Sylvan Team

Sylvan Learning Center.
Unleash your child's potential here.

No matter how big or small the academic challenge, every child has the ability to learn. But sometimes children need help making it happen. Sylvan believes every child has the potential to do great things. And, we know better than anyone else how to tap into that academic potential so that a child's future really is full of possibilities. Sylvan Learning Center is the place where your child can build and master the learning skills needed to succeed and unlock the potential you know is there.

The proven, personalized approach of our in-center programs deliver unparalleled results that other supplemental education services simply can't match. Your child's achievements will be seen not only in test scores and report cards but outside the classroom as well. And when he starts achieving his full potential, everyone will know it. You will see a new level of confidence come through in everything he does and every interaction he has.

How can Sylvan's personalized in-center approach help your child unleash his potential?

• Starting with our exclusive Sylvan Skills Assessment®, we pinpoint your child's exact academic needs.

• Then we develop a customized learning plan designed to achieve your child's academic goals.

• Through our method of skill mastery, your child will not only learn and master every skill in his personalized plan, he will be truly motivated and inspired to achieve his full potential.

To get started, included with this Sylvan product purchase is $10 off our exclusive Sylvan Skills Assessment®. Simply use this coupon and contact your local Sylvan Learning Center to set up your appointment.

And to learn more about Sylvan and our innovative in-center programs, call 1-800-EDUCATE or visit www.educate.com. *With over 1,100 locations in North America, there is a Sylvan Learning Center near you!*

4th-Grade Spelling Success

Published in the United States by Random House, Inc., New York, and in Canada by Random House of Canada Limited, Toronto.

www.tutoring.sylvanlearning.com

Created by Smarterville Productions LLC
Cover and Interior Photos: Jonathan Pozniak
Cover and Interior Illustrations: Duendes del Sur

First Edition

ISBN: 978-0-375-43004-6

Library of Congress Cataloging-in-Publication Data available upon request.

This book is available at special discounts for bulk purchases for sales promotions or premiums. For more information, write to Special Markets/Premium Sales, 1745 Broadway, MD 6-2, New York, New York 10019 or e-mail specialmarkets@randomhouse.com.

PRINTED IN CHINA

10 9 8 7 6 5 4 3 2 1

Contents

Checking your answers is part of the learning.

Each section of the workbook begins with an easy-to-use Check It! strip.

1. Before beginning the activities, cut out the Check It! strip.

2. As you complete the activities on each page, check your answers.

3. If you find an error, you can correct it yourself.

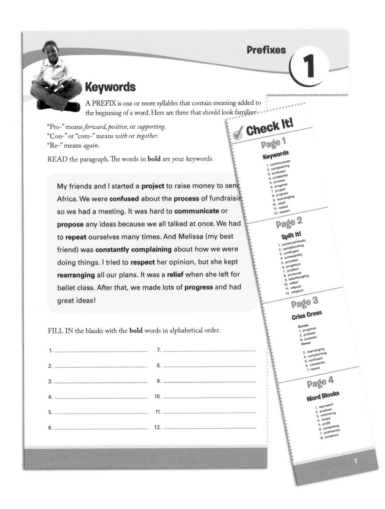

Keywords

A PREFIX is one or more syllables that contain meaning added to the beginning of a word. Here are three that should look familiar:

"Pro-" means *forward*, *positive*, or *supporting*.
"Con-" or "com-" means *with* or *together*.
"Re-" means *again*.

READ the paragraph. The words in **bold** are your keywords.

My friends and I started a **project** to raise money to send to Africa. We were **confused** about the **process** of fundraising, so we had a meeting. It was hard to **communicate** or **propose** any ideas because we all talked at once. We had to **repeat** ourselves many times. And Melissa (my best friend) was **constantly complaining** about how we were doing things. I tried to **respect** her opinion, but she kept **rearranging** all our plans. It was a **relief** when she left for ballet class. After that, we made lots of **progress** and had great ideas!

FILL IN the blanks with the **bold** words in alphabetical order.

1. _____
2. _____
3. _____
4. _____
5. _____
6. _____
7. _____
8. _____
9. _____
10. _____
11. _____
12. _____

✓ **Check It!**

Page 1

Keywords

1. communicate
2. complaining
3. confused
4. constantly
5. process
6. progress
7. project
8. propose
9. rearranging
10. relief
11. repeat
12. respect

Page 2

Split It!

1. com•mu•ni•cate
2. com•plain•ing
3. con•fused
4. con•stant•ly
5. proc•ess
6. prog•ress
7. proj•ect
8. pro•pose
9. re•ar•rang•ing
10. re•lief
11. re•peat
12. re•spect

Page 3

Criss Cross

Across
1. progress
3. process
8. propose
Down

2. rearranging
4. complaining
5. confused
6. constantly
7. repeat

Page 4

Word Blocks

1. represent
2. produce
3. reminding
4. renew
5. profit
6. competing
7. pronounce
8. construct

Split It!

SPLIT these keywords into syllables, using dots to mark the breaks.

HINT: A prefix is usually its own syllable. Also, when a syllable ends in a LONG vowel sound, it usually ends with a vowel, like this: *pa•per*.

TIP: You usually use "com-" when the next letter is "p," "m," or "b."

Example: control   con•trol

communicate	1. _____
complaining	2. _____
confused	3. _____
constantly	4. _____
process	5. _____
progress	6. _____
project	7. _____
propose	8. _____
rearranging	9. _____
relief	10. _____
repeat	11. _____
respect	12. _____

Criss Cross

FILL IN the grid by answering the clues with keywords.

ACROSS

1. Improvement

3. Method or system

8. Suggest an idea

DOWN

2. Putting things in a different order

4. Whining

5. Puzzled

6. Something that never stops is done…

7. To say again

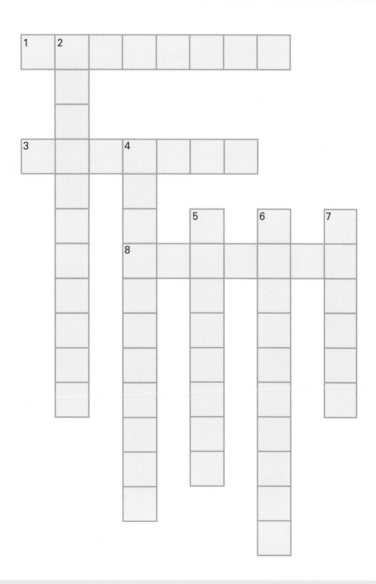

Word Blocks

FILL IN the blanks with "com" or "con," "re," or "pro" to make the correct word. Then FILL IN the word blocks with words of the same shape.

Example: That show is a <u>re</u>peat. I've seen it before!

I went to the library to ____new the books I haven't finished yet.

The candy costs us $1 and we sell it for $2. That's a dollar ____fit!

My art class is working together to ____struct a tower out of toothpicks.

How do you ____nounce the word *anemone*?

We sent Jeremiah to the coach so he could ____present the team.

With a little help, I can ____duce ten chocolate cream pies a day!

Our tennis team is ____peting in a major tournament.

Thanks for ____minding me about the sneaker sale!

Word Search

FILL IN the blanks with "com" or "con," "re," or "pro" to make the correct word. Then CIRCLE the words in the word grid. Words go down and across, not diagonally or backwards.

Example: It's a <u>relief</u> to drop my heavy backpack!

1. I broke Mrs. Arora's window and had to pay to get it ____paired.

2. All the band members have their names listed in the ____gram.

3. That house isn't made of brick. It's made of ____crete blocks.

4. It's hard to ____pare Superman with Batman. They're very different.

5. My brother and I are staging a ____test against broccoli. Join us!

6. The YMCA will ____vide towels if you want to swim.

7. Mickey won the burping ____test again. He's the best burper in town.

8. My sister is in love with her college history ____fessor. Yuck!

9. It took me two weeks to ____cover from the flu.

10. My parents are trying to ____vince me to clean the garage. Yeah, right.

W	P	M	C	Z	R	K	P	P	E	R
C	R	X	O	W	E	C	R	R	X	E
O	O	P	M	C	L	O	U	O	R	P
N	G	R	P	O	I	N	C	T	E	A
V	R	O	A	N	E	T	L	E	C	I
I	A	P	R	O	F	E	S	S	O	R
N	M	F	E	R	E	S	W	T	V	E
C	O	N	C	R	E	T	E	B	E	D
E	Q	P	R	O	V	I	D	E	R	P

Match Up

Here are some words that share the same ROOT, or body, but have different prefixes. MATCH the word on the left with the definition on the right. WRITE the letter of the answer in the blank.

Example: composition   putting things (like words) together in a certain way

1. reposition ____
2. retest ____
3. protest ____
4. contest ____
5. confuse ____
6. refuse ____
7. contract ____
8. retract ____
9. protract ____

a. an agreement between people
b. to test again
c. to take back
d. make longer, draw out
e. to put in a different place
f. a competition
g. to disagree
h. garbage (or to say *no*)
i. to puzzle or cause doubt

 **Check It!**

Cut out the Check It! section on page 1, and see if you got the answers right.

Keywords

Did you know that there are lots of prefixes that mean *not*? Here are a few:

"non-" as in *nonfat*

"in-" and "im-" as in *incorrect* and *impossible*

"dis-" as in *disagree*

READ the paragraph. The words in **bold** are your keywords.

It's very **immature** to act badly on an airplane. Kicking the seat in front of you is totally **impolite**. And you shouldn't be **disrespectful** of the flight attendants or **disobey** their orders. They **disapprove** of that kind of **nonsense**. Last time I flew, I only brought one **nonfiction** book to read. Luckily, it was a **nonstop** flight. An **indirect** flight, with stops along the way, would have been **inexpensive**, but also **inconvenient** and longer. I was **impatient** to be on the ground again!

FILL IN the blanks with the **bold** words in alphabetical order.

1. _____

2. _____

3. _____

4. _____

5. _____

6. _____

7. _____

8. _____

9. _____

10. _____

11. _____

12. _____

✓ Check It!

Page 7

Keywords

1. disapprove
2. disobey
3. disrespectful
4. immature
5. impatient
6. impolite
7. inconvenient
8. indirect
9. inexpensive
10. nonfiction
11. nonsense
12. nonstop

Page 8

Stack Up

2-Syllable Words
1. nonsense
2. nonstop

4-Syllable Words
1. inexpensive
2. disrespectful
3. inconvenient

3-Syllable Words
1. impatient
2. immature
3. disobey
4. nonfiction
5. indirect
6. disapprove
7. impolite

Page 9

Word Search

N	O	N	F	I	C	T	I	O	N
E	X	P	E	N	S	I	V	E	O
N	D	A	Z	D	W	M	U	M	N
O	I	T	D	I	S	D	P	X	S
I	S	I	M	R	V	I	O	Y	E
S	O	E	W	E	K	S	L	Q	N
T	B	N	D	C	Y	X	I	I	S
O	E	T	R	T	N	T	T	M	E
P	Y	M	A	T	U	R	E	U	N
C	O	N	V	E	N	I	E	N	T

Page 10

Spotlight on "Un-"

1. unwilling
2. undecided
3. unfamiliar
4. unpopular
5. unemployed
6. unripe
7. ungrateful
8. unimportant
9. unpleasant
10. unnatural

Bonus:
1. uncomfortable
2. discomfort
3. unarmed
4. disarm

Stack Up

READ the keywords out loud. SORT them by the number of syllables. FILL IN the blanks with the sorted words.

TIP: Use the "im-" prefix with words that start with "m" or "p."

impatient	immature	disobey	nonfiction
inexpensive	nonsense	indirect	disapprove
disrespectful	inconvenient	nonstop	impolite

2-Syllable Words
Example: nonfat

1. _____

2. _____

4-Syllable Words
Example: impossible

1. _____

2. _____

3. _____

3-Syllable Words
Example: incorrect

1. _____

2. _____

3. _____

4. _____

5. _____

6. _____

7. _____

Word Search

FILL IN the blanks with keywords and their opposites. Then CIRCLE the words underlined in blue in the word grid. Words go down and across, not diagonally or backwards.

Example: If <u>polite</u> *means* being nice, *then* <u>impolite</u> *means* being rude.

1. If _____ means *costly*, then _____ means *cheap*.

2. If _____ means *willing to wait*, then _____ means *unable to wait*.

3. If _____ means *straightforward*, then _____ means *not straightforward*.

4. If _____ is *a story that isn't true*, then _____ is *a true story*.

5. If _____ means *grownup*, then _____ means *childish*.

6. If _____ means *easy*, then _____ means *difficult*.

7. If _____ means *to take a break*, then _____ means *to keep going*.

8. If _____ means *to follow orders*, then _____ means *to break the rules*.

9. If _____ means *intelligence*, then _____ is *silliness*.

N	O	N	F	I	C	T	I	O	N
E	X	P	E	N	S	I	V	E	O
N	D	A	Z	D	W	M	U	M	N
O	I	T	D	I	S	D	P	X	S
N	S	I	M	R	V	I	O	Y	E
S	O	E	W	E	K	S	L	Q	N
T	B	N	D	C	Y	X	I	I	S
O	E	T	R	T	N	T	T	M	E
P	Y	M	A	T	U	R	E	U	N
C	O	N	V	E	N	I	E	N	T

Spotlight on "Un-"

Guess what? There's another prefix that means *not*. ADD the prefix "un-" to each new word. FILL IN the blanks with the right "un-" word.

civilized	decided	employed	familiar	grateful	important
natural	pleasant	popular	ripe	welcome	willing

1. Chad will not shower no matter what. He's totally _____.

2. Vicki hasn't chosen a skirt yet. She's still _____.

3. I've never been on this block before. It's _____.

4. Someone with zero friends is very _____.

5. Don't have a job? Then you're _____.

6. A fruit that's not ready to eat is _____.

7. If you can't say, "thank you," then you're _____.

8. A clean shirt is _____ to me, but my mom feels differently.

9. Aunt Trudy thinks the Crawfords are _____ because they're loud.

10. A baby duck with three heads? That's _____!

Bonus

There are times when "dis-" and "un-" share a word. FILL IN the blank with "dis-" or "un-" to make the right word.

1. This hard chair is _____comfortable.

2. My _____comfort is caused by this hard chair.

3. That man has no weapons, so he is _____armed.

4. If he had weapons and you took them away, you would _____arm him.

Pick the One!

CIRCLE the word that uses the right prefix.

Not a believer	1.	inbeliever	nonbeliever
Not perfect	2.	inperfect	imperfect
Not active	3.	inactive	imactive
Not a member	4.	unmember	nonmember
Not certain	5.	uncertain	incertain
Not appearing anymore	6.	disappearing	unappearing
Not pure	7.	inpure	impure
Not authorized	8.	inauthorized	unauthorized
Not existent	9.	inexistent	nonexistent
Not practical	10.	inpractical	impractical
Not definite	11.	indefinite	imdefinite
Not toxic	12.	untoxic	nontoxic
Not human	13.	inhuman	dishuman
Not approving	14.	disapproving	inapproving
Not personal	15.	nonpersonal	impersonal
Not familiar	16.	infamiliar	unfamiliar
Not honest	17.	dishonest	unhonest
Not limited	18.	dislimited	unlimited
Not sane	19.	insane	nonsane
Not seen	20.	unseen	nonseen
Not sincere	21.	insincere	imsincere
Not scientific	22.	inscientific	unscientific
Not a swimmer	23.	inswimmer	nonswimmer
Not welcome	24.	unwelcome	diswelcome

Split It!

SPLIT these words into syllables, using dots to mark the breaks.

HINT: A prefix is usually its own syllable.

Example: incorrect   in•cor•rect

disobey	1. _____
disrespect	2. _____
disapprove	3. _____
immature	4. _____
impatient	5. _____
impersonal	6. _____
inconvenient	7. _____
indirect	8. _____
inexpensive	9. _____
informal	10. _____
inhuman	11. _____
nonfiction	12. _____
nonprofit	13. _____
nonsense	14. _____
unbroken	15. _____

Check It!

Cut out the Check It! section on page 7, and see if you got the answers right.

Keywords

Here are a few more prefixes for your brain to chew on:

"Fore-" means *before* or *in front*, as in *foresee*.
"En-" or "em-" means *in*, *on*, or *to make*, as in *enrage*.

READ the paragraph. The words in **bold** are your keywords.

> The weather **forecast** called for rain, so we went to the museum. In the **foreground** of one painting, there was a man with his hands on his **forehead** and a ring on his **forefinger**. He was **enclosed** in a cage and he looked really angry. The painting was **entitled** "**Enraged** Man **Entrapped** in Cage." I learned that the artist was **unemployed** when he painted this. But it **empowered** his career, making him the **foremost** artist of his time and **enriching** him beyond his wildest dreams!

FILL IN the blanks with the **bold** words in alphabetical order.

1. _____
2. _____
3. _____
4. _____
5. _____
6. _____
7. _____
8. _____
9. _____
10. _____
11. _____
12. _____

Check It!

Page 13

Keywords

1. empowered
2. enclosed
3. enraged
4. enriching
5. entitled
6. entrapped
7. forecast
8. forefinger
9. foreground
10. forehead
11. foremost
12. unemployed

Page 14

Split It!

1. em•ploy
2. em•pow•er
3. en•close
4. en•rage
5. en•rich
6. en•ti•tle
7. en•trap
8. fore•cast
9. fore•fin•ger
10. fore•ground
11. fore•head
12. fore•most

Page 15

Criss Cross

Across
1. foremost
3. foreground
4. enraged
6. enriching

Down
1. forehead
2. empowered
3. forefinger
5. entitled

Page 16

Word Blocks

1. preschool
2. forelegs
3. precaution
4. preview
5. prepay
6. forearm

✓ Check It!

Page 17

Pick the One!

1. enlarge
2. embrace
3. foresee
4. entrust
5. employ
6. preheat
7. endanger
8. forethought
9. empower
10. preexist
11. foreman
12. prearrange
13. encircle

Page 18

Blank Out!

1. entangle
2. forewarned
3. revision
4. encourage
5. premature
6. profile
7. nonsmoking
8. dissatisified
9. insecure
10. discourage
11. disorder
12. contribute

Split It!

SPLIT these keywords into syllables, using dots to mark the breaks.

HINT: A prefix (or a suffix) is usually its own syllable.

TIP: Use the "em-" prefix with words that start with "b" or "p."

employ	1. _____
empower	2. _____
enclose	3. _____
enrage	4. _____
enrich	5. _____
entitle	6. _____
entrap	7. _____
forecast	8. _____
forefinger	9. _____
foreground	10. _____
forehead	11. _____
foremost	12. _____

Criss Cross

FILL IN the grid by answering the clues with keywords.

ACROSS

1. The very first

3. The front part of a picture, closest to you

4. Put in a rage

6. Making rich

DOWN

1. The front of your head

2. Made more powerful

3. Your front finger

5. Made or gave a title

Word Blocks

Don't forget the prefix "pre-," which, like "fore-," means *before* or *first*.

FILL IN the blanks with either "fore" or "pre" to make the correct word. Then, FILL IN the word blocks with words of the same shape. Be sure to include the prefix.

Example: The label says to precook the meat first.

My sister has a scar on the front part of her arm, her _____arm.

Arnold's Dad got us tickets to a _____view of the next Disney movie.

Kids who are too young for kindergarten go to _____school.

When an animal has four legs, the front ones are called the _____legs.

As a _____caution, make sure you have your cell phone.

When you buy movie tickets online, you have to _____pay.

Pick the One!

CIRCLE the word that uses the correct prefix.

Example: To put in code (encode) *emcode*

Make large	1. enlarge	emlarge
Enclose in your arms	2. enbrace	embrace
See something before it happens	3. foresee	presee
Put your trust in	4. entrust	emtrust
Make use of, to hire	5. enploy	employ
Heat up beforehand	6. foreheat	preheat
Put in danger	7. endanger	emdanger
A thought beforehand	8. forethought	prethought
Make more powerful	9. enpower	empower
Exist before	10. foreexist	preexist
The lead man on a job	11. foreman	preman
Arrange ahead of time	12. forearrange	prearrange
Put in a circle	13. encircle	emcircle

Blank Out!

Here are the prefixes we've covered so far: "con-," "pro-," "re-," "in-," "non-," "dis-," "un-," "fore-," "en-," and "pre-" Let's try them out on new words!

warned	secure	order	courage	vision
mature	satisfied	tribute	smoking	file

FILL IN the blanks by adding a prefix to one of the words in the box.

HINT: *Courage* is used twice.

Example: Don't drink the water here. It's totally impure.

1. Clumsy Kristy managed to _____ herself in the jump rope!

2. The smell of smoke _____ me of the fire.

3. My story wasn't funny enough, so I wrote a _____.

4. I was afraid to sing in the play, but Mom smiled to _____ me.

5. Since Ziggy's only 12, driving lessons would be _____ for him.

6. MTV played a _____ of my favorite band that had lots of information.

7. My parents always ask for a _____ room at a hotel.

8. When I miss a goal, I can tell Coach Cruz is _____.

9. Maria isn't sure about her voice, so she's _____ about singing on stage.

10. If Thom keeps losing tennis matches, it'll _____ him from playing.

11. While the men were painting, our house was in total _____.

12. Mom says everyone has to _____ to cleaning the house.

✓ Check It!

Cut out the Check It! section on page 13, and see if you got the answers right.

Keywords

We've got three shiny new prefixes to play with!

"Over-" means *too much* or *above*.
"Under-" means *below*, *lower*, or *too little*.
"Inter-" means *among*, *between*, or *together*.

READ the paragraph. The words in **bold** are your keywords.

I stayed **overnight** at my friend Cal's. He lives near the **interstate** highway. His little brother wore nothing but purple **underpants** and a shirt that said: "**Overworked** and **Underpaid**." His older brother refused to **interact** with us; he was watching a basketball game that had gone into **overtime**. Pepper, Cal's little sister, kept **interrupting** our conversation to show us stuff on the **Internet**. Dinner was completely **undercooked** and gross. Later, we tried to use Cal's new telescope, but the sky was **overcast**. I knew I wouldn't **oversleep** the next morning. I was ready to leave!

FILL IN the blanks with the **bold** words in alphabetical order.

1. _____
2. _____
3. _____
4. _____
5. _____
6. _____
7. _____
8. _____
9. _____
10. _____
11. _____
12. _____

✔ Check It!

Page 19

Keywords

1. interact
2. Internet
3. interrupting
4. interstate
5. overcast
6. overnight
7. oversleep
8. overtime
9. overworked
10. undercooked
11. underpaid
12. underpants

Page 20

Split It!

1. in•ter•act
2. In•ter•net
3. in•ter•rupt
4. in•ter•state
5. o•ver•cast
6. o•ver•night
7. o•ver•sleep
8. o•ver•time
9. o•ver•worked
10. un•der•cooked
11. un•der•paid
12. un•der•pants

Page 21

Word Search

X	I	O	V	E	R	T	I	M	E	Q	N	R
U	N	D	E	R	C	O	O	K	E	D	I	I
N	T	O	O	V	R	V	U	N	D	I	N	T
D	E	V	U	N	D	E	R	P	A	N	T	S
E	R	E	O	V	E	R	W	O	R	K	E	D
R	A	R	I	N	T	S	Y	I	M	E	R	Y
P	C	C	U	N	D	L	P	A	N	X	N	I
A	T	A	L	R	W	E	O	O	F	B	E	N
I	F	S	I	N	T	E	R	R	U	P	T	T
D	G	T	O	V	E	P	X	Q	V	R	C	W

Page 22

Spotlight

1. underline
2. submarine
3. underwater
4. submit
5. underside
6. subway
7. subtitle
8. suburb
9. subzero
10. undershirt
11. subject
12. underground
13. subhuman
14. subtract

Prefixes Everywhere!

Split It!

SPLIT the keywords into syllables, using dots to mark the breaks.

HINT: Here's how to split the prefixes: o•ver   un•der   in•ter
Example: understand   un•der•stand

interact

Internet

interrupt

interstate

overcast

overnight

oversleep

overtime

overworked

undercooked

underpaid

underpants

1. _____

2. _____

3. _____

4. _____

5. _____

6. _____

7. _____

8. _____

9. _____

10. _____

11. _____

12. _____

Word Search

FILL IN the blanks with keywords. Then CIRCLE the words in the word grid. Words go down and across, not diagonally or backwards.

1. My brother gets paid extra when he works _____.

2. Dad made me clean the garage all day! I'm totally _____.

3. The old lady next door lives alone and doesn't _____ with anybody.

4. My computer's got a really fast _____ connection.

5. Are these beans _____ or are they supposed to be frozen?

6. Tyrell has a loud alarm clock so he won't _____.

7. In my dream, I was walking down the street in just my _____!

8. Sunny days are too hot! I like when the sky's a little _____.

9. Don't _____ me! Let me finish my speech!

10. Zella only gets $3 an hour? She's really _____.

X	I	O	V	E	R	T	I	M	E	Q	N	R
U	N	D	E	R	C	O	O	K	E	D	I	I
N	T	O	O	V	R	V	U	N	D	I	N	T
D	E	V	U	N	D	E	R	P	A	N	T	S
E	R	E	O	V	E	R	W	O	R	K	E	D
R	A	R	I	N	T	S	Y	I	M	E	R	Y
P	C	C	U	N	D	L	P	A	N	X	N	I
A	T	A	L	R	W	E	O	O	F	B	E	N
I	F	S	I	N	T	E	R	R	U	P	T	T
D	G	T	O	V	E	P	X	Q	V	R	C	W

Spotlight on "Sub-"

"Sub-" is another prefix that means *under* or *less than*.

READ each sentence. UNSCRAMBLE the **bold** word.
FILL IN the blanks with the unscrambled words.

HINT: All of the words start with the prefix "sub-"
or "under-."

I always **reeduniln** my name when I sign notes.

If you had a **serabimun**, you could go deep under the ocean.

Walt wants to build an **wretunerda** city. He likes fish!

To join the club, you have to **tumbis** a form online.

Garrett put stickers on the **sidderune** of his skateboard.

We took the **wabusy** to the Central Park Zoo.

The **buttelis** of this book is *A True Story*.

We live in a **rubbus** of Chicago.

We get **bezrous** temperatures here every winter!

Dad wears an **thirsderun** beneath his fancy shirts.

Don't talk about frogs! That's a forbidden **jebcust**.

The train goes **gerruddounn** through a tunnel.

Lydia doesn't like me. She treats me like I'm **baushnum**.

Mom will **cattrubs** a dollar from my allowance if
I skip a chore.

1. _____

2. _____

3. _____

4. _____

5. _____

6. _____

7. _____

8. _____

9. _____

10. _____

11. _____

12. _____

13. _____

14. _____

Pick the One!

CIRCLE the word with the correct prefix.

Not weighing enough	1. subweight	underweight
Involving two or more nations	2. undernational	international
Below ground	3. underground	interground
On the other side of the ocean	4. overseas	underseas
A ship that goes deep under water	5. undermarine	submarine
A line beneath some words	6. overline	underline
Translate between languages	7. overterpret	interpret
Too full	8. overloaded	underloaded
Divide into smaller parts	9. underdivide	subdivide
Eat too much	10. overeat	intereat
Below the water	11. underwater	interwater
A town outside a city	12 interurb	suburb
Dressed too formally	13. overdressed	underdressed
The bottom side	14. overside	underside
Where two streets come together	15. subsection	intersection
A coat you wear on top of your clothes	16. overcoat	undercoat
Less than normal	17. undernormal	subnormal
To get in the middle	18. underfere	interfere
Where a street crosses above another street	19. overpass	underpass
Do too much	20. overdo	underdo

Stack Up

SORT the words in the box into the categories. FILL IN the blanks with the sorted words, including the prefixes.

HINT: Some words can be used with more than one prefix. Say each word with each prefix. Does it sound right?

face	ground	hear	load	look	marine	mission	national
rule	stand	taking	turn	title	total	water	

Words That Go with "Under-"
Example: underwear

1. _____

2. _____

3. _____

4. _____

Words That Go with "Over-"
Example: overweight

1. _____

2. _____

3. _____

4. _____

5. _____

6. _____

Words That Go with "Sub-"
Example: subway

1. _____

2. _____

3. _____

4. _____

Words That Go with "Inter-"
Example: internet

1. _____

2. _____

3. _____

 Check It!

Cut out Check It! to see if you got the answers right.

Keywords

Do you have room for three more prefixes?

"Semi-" means *half* or *moderately*, like *semicircle*, which is half of a circle.
"Anti-" means *against* or *opposite*, like *antiwar*.
"Multi-" means *much* or *many*, like *multicolor*.

READ the paragraph. The words in **bold** are your keywords.

Uh-oh. Mom has her **semiannual** cold. She's taking **antibiotics** and a bunch of **multivitamins**. She sits on the couch all day, wrapped in a **multicolored** blanket, with a **multitude** of magazines and tissues in a **semicircle** in front of her. When I asked if I could watch the basketball **semifinals** in the living room, she said no. She gets so **antisocial** when she's sick! Meanwhile, Dad is writing an **antiwar** article for a **multinational** magazine. He's stinky, because he forgets to wear **antiperspirant**. All he thinks about are commas and **semicolons**. I'm living in a nuthouse!

FILL IN the blanks with the **bold** words in alphabetical order.

1. _____
2. _____
3. _____
4. _____
5. _____
6. _____

7. _____
8. _____
9. _____
10. _____
11. _____
12. _____

Multiprefixed!

Split It!

SPLIT the keywords into syllables, using dots to mark the breaks.

HINT: Here's how to split the prefixes:

an•ti   mul•ti   sem•i

Example: multiply   mul•ti•ply

antibiotics	1. _____
antiperspirant	2. _____
antisocial	3. _____
antiwar	4. _____
multicolored	5. _____
multinational	6. _____
multitude	7. _____
multivitamins	8. _____
semiannual	9. _____
semicircle	10. _____
semicolons	11. _____
semifinals	12. _____

✓ Check It!

Page 29

Pick the One!

1. antifreeze	10. semisoft
2. semitropical	11. misuse
3. misspelled	12. semiprecious
4. multicultural	13. multimedia
5. antislavery	14. mismatched
6. antiperspirant	15. semisolid
7. semimonthly	16. misunderstood
8. mistyped	17. antidote
9. multipurpose	18. multiplies

Page 30

Author! Author!

Check to be sure you used six of the words. Then look them up in a dictionary to see if you used them correctly.

Criss Cross

FILL IN the grid by answering the clues with keywords.

ACROSS

2. Half comma, half colon

3. Has many colors

4. Of many countries

5. Prevents sweaty armpits

6. Drugs that fight infections

DOWN

1. Halfway through the finals

3. A pill containing many vitamins

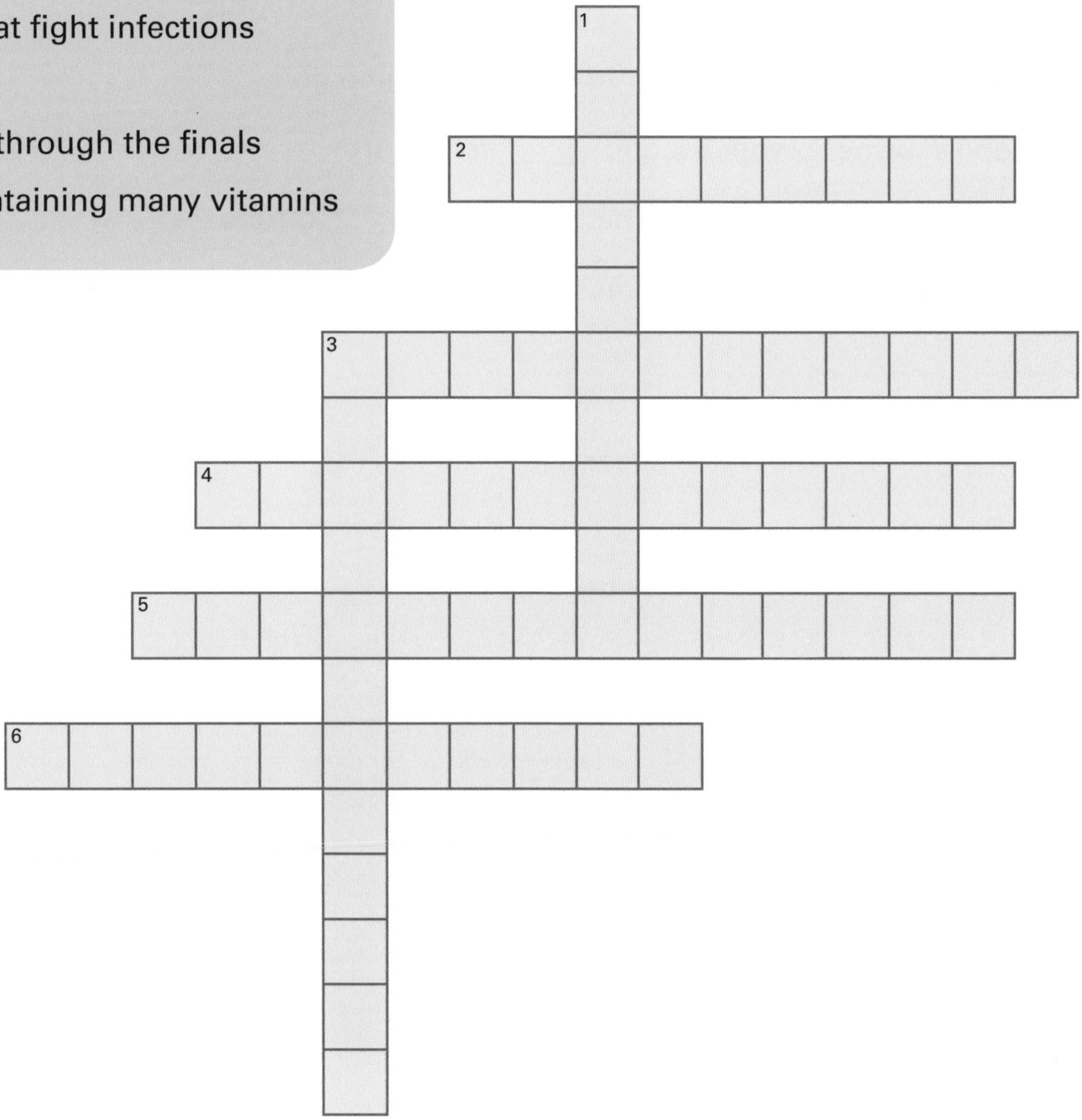

Word Blocks

Don't forget the prefix "mis-," which means *wrong*. It's easy to confuse it with "anti-," which means *against* or *opposite*.

FILL IN the blanks with either "anti" or "mis" to make the correct word.
Then FILL IN the word blocks with words of the same shape. Be sure to include the prefix.

Example: Why does everyone misspell my name?

Marsha's great-great-grandpa was part of the _____ slavery movement.

The paper said I won the lottery, but that was a _____ print!

We put _____ freeze in the car to keep the engine going.

Our dog's former owner used to _____ treat him.

You lost everything in a fire? That's a major _____ fortune!

Where are my headphones? I must have _____ placed them.

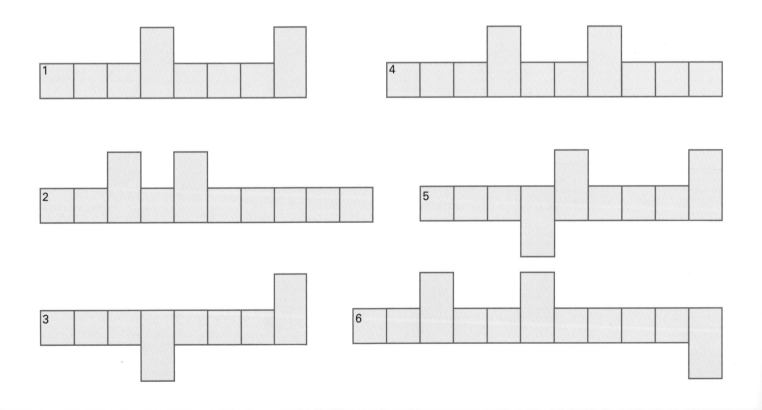

Pick the One!

CIRCLE the word with the correct prefix.

Keeps things from freezing	1. misfreeze	antifreeze
Moderately tropical	2. semitropical	multitropical
Spelled wrong	3. misspelled	antispelled
Of many cultures	4. semicultural	multicultural
Against slavery	5. multislavery	antislavery
Stops perspiration	6. misperspirant	antiperspirant
Twice a month	7. semimonthly	multimonthly
Typed wrong	8. semityped	mistyped
Has many purposes	9. semipurpose	multipurpose
Moderately soft	10. semisoft	multisoft
Put to the wrong use	11. misuse	semiuse
Moderately precious	12 semiprecious	misprecious
Uses many kinds of media	13. semimedia	multimedia
Matched incorrectly	14. mismatched	antimatched
Not quite solid	15. semisolid	antisolid
Understood the wrong thing	16. misunderstood	semiunderstood
Something that prevents poisoning	17. misdote	antidote
Makes many more	18. semiplies	multiplies

Author! Author!

It's your turn to do the writing. Use at least six of the new words to write a story, a poem, or a list of crazy sentences. Have fun!

insane	nonstop	disappear	imperfect	unpopular	forecast
prehistoric	enrich	embrace	overboard	underwear	submarine

_____

_____

_____

_____

_____

_____

_____

_____

_____

_____

_____

_____

_____

 **Check It!**

Cut out Check It! to see if you got the answers right.

Spell Check

READ each sentence. CIRCLE the word that has the wrong prefix. FILL IN the blanks with the correct words. Use the right prefixes!

Example: Fluffy likes to ⟨underact⟩ with other dogs.   *interact*

1. I can be shy, so I feel unsecure at parties.

2. Cindy used my computer and misorganized my files.

3. It would be inpractical to fly. Let's take the train.

4. Mom left a note to commind me to bring my lunch.

5. Being captain would enpower you to set the batting order.

6. Check the weather precast before the picnic.

7. Don't indanger yourself by crossing against the light.

8. I'm at the undersection of 4th and Main. Where are you?

9. Ew! I saw Dad in his subpants today.

1. _____

2. _____

3. _____

4. _____

5. _____

6. _____

7. _____

8. _____

9. _____

Criss Cross

FILL IN each blank with the right prefix to finish the word.
WRITE the words in the grid.

ACROSS

4. Twice a year, our church has its _____annual bingo night.

6. The horse lost a shoe on her _____leg, not her back one.

7. Shira tries to _____tect her little sister from bullies.

DOWN

1. Kara _____read the flyer and went to the wrong store.

2. My parents are religious, but Grandpa is a _____believer.

3. My karate class is _____racial, with kids from all over.

5. It's _____

Word Blocks

ADD the correct prefix to make the opposite of the words listed. FILL IN the word blocks with the new words of the same shape.

HINT: Use one of the "not" prefixes: in-/im-, non-, dis-, or un-.

Example: willing   unwilling

action _____

toxic _____

direct _____

agree _____

visible _____

correct _____

natural _____

patient _____

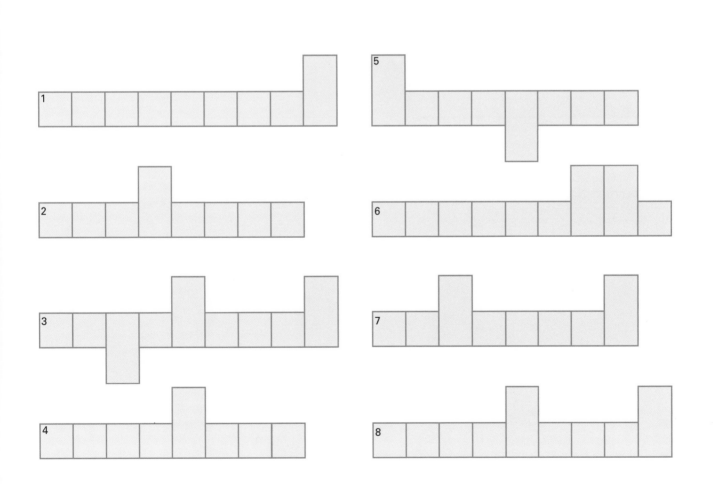

Stack Up

A PREFIX is not usually a word by itself. A COMPOUND WORD is a word that's made of two words stuck together. Can you tell the difference?

SORT the words by category.

composition	bridesmaid	courtroom	discontinue
everybody	forecast	gentleman	lightweight
misplace	proclaim	screwdriver	understand

Compound Words

Example: highway

1. _____
2. _____
3. _____
4. _____
5. _____
6. _____

Words with Prefixes

Example: misspell

1. _____
2. _____
3. _____
4. _____
5. _____
6. _____

 **Check It!**

Cut out Check It! to see if you got the answers right.

Meet the Suffixes

6

Keywords

A SUFFIX is an ending added to a word that changes its meaning. Here are a few for starters:

"-Y" turns *trick* (noun) to *tricky* (adjective).
"-Ly" turns *sad* (adjective) to *sadly* (adverb).
"-Er" and "-or" turn *act* (verb) to *actor* (noun).
"-Ness" turns *happy* (adjective) to *happiness* (noun).

READ the paragraph. The words in **bold** are your keywords.

> In my family, I'm the **brainy** one, and my sister, Isabella, is the performer. She practices skating every **frosty** winter morning with an **instructor** at the rink in town. You may think that's **crazy**, but in competition, Isabelle defeats every **challenger** with **perfectly** executed moves that show the **thoroughness** of her training. Once we watched **anxiously** as she leaped into a triple axle. She landed it **flawlessly**! My sister's **seriousness** about ice skating keeps her really busy, which means a little **loneliness** for me. But that's okay. She says I can be her **manager** one day!

FILL IN the blanks with the **bold** words in alphabetical order.

1. _____
2. _____
3. _____
4. _____
5. _____
6. _____
7. _____
8. _____
9. _____
10. _____
11. _____
12. _____

✓ Check It!

Page 35
Keywords
1. anxiously
2. brainy
3. challenger
4. crazy
5. flawlessly
6. frosty
7. instructor
8. loneliness
9. manager
10. perfectly
11. seriousness
12. thoroughness

Page 36
Stack Up

Nouns	Adverbs
1. challenger	1. anxiously
2. instructor	2. flawlessly
3. loneliness	3. perfectly
4. manager	
5. seriousness	**Adjectives**
6. thoroughness	1. brainy
	2. crazy
	3. frosty

Page 37
Alternate Endings

Adjective (+ "-y")	Adverb (+ "-ly")
1. itchy	itchily
2. gloomy	gloomily
3. grumpy	grumpily
4. moody	moodily
5. worthy	worthily
6. frosty	frostily
7. scratch	scratchily

Bonus:
1. breezy	breezily
2. slimy	slimily
3. crazy	crazily

Page 38
Morph It!
1. preacher
2. forecaster
3. babysitter
4. entertainer
5. manager
6. hairdresser
7. troublemaker
8. screwdriver
9. showstopper

Bonus:
1. protector
2. instructor
3. investigator
4. sculptor

35

Stack Up

READ the keywords out loud. SORT them into the categories.

anxiously	brainy	challenger	crazy
flawlessly	frosty	instructor	loneliness
manager	perfectly	seriousness	thoroughness

Nouns
Examples: sadness, teacher

1. _____
2. _____
3. _____
4. _____
5. _____
6. _____

Adverbs
Example: happily

1. _____
2. _____
3. _____

Adjectives
Example: tricky

1. _____
2. _____
3. _____

Alternate Endings

When a word ends in "y," change the "y" to an "i" before adding the suffix: *merry, merrily, merriness.*

ADD suffixes to these words to make them into adjectives and adverbs.

HINT: Change the "y" to an "i" before changing the adjectives into adverbs.

Example: trick   tricky   trickily

Noun	Adjective (+ "-y")	Adverb (+ "-ly")
itch	1. _____	_____
gloom	2. _____	_____
grump	3. _____	_____
mood	4. _____	_____
worth	5. _____	_____
frost	6. _____	_____
scratch	7. _____	_____

Bonus

When a word ends in "e," you usually drop the "e" before adding the "y" or "ly."

Example: bounce   bouncy   bouncily

Noun	Adjective	Adverb
breeze	1. _____	_____
slime	2. _____	_____
craze	3. _____	_____

Morph It!

Did you know that the suffix "-er" can turn a verb into a noun? Well, now you do. FILL IN the blanks by adding the suffix "-er" to make the **bold** verb into a noun.

TIP: When a word ends in one vowel followed by one consonant (like *bag*), you usually have to double the consonant before the suffix.

*Example: A person who **bags** groceries is a **bagger**.*

1. Mr. McDonald **preaches** sermons, so he's a _____.

2. On TV, Lizzie Winters does the noon **forecast**. She's a weather _____.

3. Theresa **babysits** her brother. She's a _____.

4. Ricky **entertains** us with his jokes. Someday, he'll be an _____.

5. My uncle **manages** a candy store. He's a store _____.

6. Michael **dresses** up Mom's hair for special nights. He's a hair_____.

7. Since Lucy is always **making** trouble, Mom calls her a trouble_____.

8. The tool you use to **drive** in a screw is a screw_____.

9. An act that **stops** the show is a show_____.

Bonus

Add "-or" to the **bold** words to make them into people.
HINT: If a verb ends in an "e," drop the "e" before you add the ending.

1. If you **protect** someone, you're his _____.

2. Ilia **instructs** me in Spanish. She's an _____.

3. Mr. Garbo **investigates** crime. He's an _____.

4. Wow, the person who **sculpted** that statue is a great _____.

Spotlight on "-Ful" and "-Less"

Here are two more suffixes that are really useful to know!
"-Ful" means full of, so *useful* means *full of use*.
"-Less" means lacking, so *useless* means *has no use*.

FILL IN the blanks to match the clues.

Example: Full of use   useful

Clue	
Full of sorrow	1. _____
Lacking any flaw	2. _____
Full of plenty	3. _____
Has no doubt	4. _____
Full of delight	5. _____
Lacking breath	6. _____
With no effort	7. _____
Full of bounty	8. _____
Has no humor	9. _____
Full of disgrace	10. _____
Not able to rest	11. _____
Full of flavor	12. _____
Has no weapon	13. _____
Full of meaning	14. _____
Lacking worth	15. _____
Full of scorn	16. _____

Alternate Endings Again!

ADD "-less" to the nouns to make them adjectives.
ADD "-ness" to the adjectives to make them nouns.
SPLIT the new words into syllables, using dots to mark the breaks.

HINT: A suffix is usually its own syllable. Some words have more than one suffix!

Example: joy   joy•less   useful   use•ful•ness

polite	1. _____
kind	2. _____
home	3. _____
cloud	4. _____
good	5. _____
spot	6. _____
sweet	7. _____
spine	8. _____
fit	9. _____
careless	10. _____
thoughtful	11. _____
cheer	12. _____
painless	13. _____
hopeful	14. _____
thoughtless	15. _____
youthful	16. _____

Keywords

You've seen how the suffixes "-er" and "-or" can turn a verb like *teach* into a noun like *teacher*. Here are two more suffixes that do the same thing!

"-Ment" turns *amaze* into *amazement*.

"-Ion" turns *act* into *action*.

READ the paragraph. The words in **bold** are your keywords.

Music is my life! I love to sing while my brother plays the **accompaniment** on his guitar. My **ambition** is to find **employment** as a musician. I could also give **instruction** to kids, write my own **composition** and **arrangement** of songs, and maybe even star in a musical **production**! My teacher has seen a lot of **improvement** in my work since I made the **commitment** to practice every day. Yesterday, I received an **invitation** to a major singing **competition**! I can barely handle the **excitement**!

FILL IN the blanks with the **bold** words in alphabetical order.

1. _____
2. _____
3. _____
4. _____
5. _____
6. _____
7. _____
8. _____
9. _____
10. _____
11. _____
12. _____

 **Check It!**

Page 41
Keywords

1. accompaniment
2. ambition
3. arrangement
4. commitment
5. competition
6. composition
7. employment
8. excitement
9. improvement
10. instruction
11. invitation
12. production

Page 42
Morph It!

1. accompaniment
2. arrangement
3. commitment
4. competition
5. composition
6. employment
7. excitement
8. improvement
9. instruction
10. invitation
11. production

Page 43
Alternate Endings

1. excitement
2. punishment
3. adoption
4. amusement
5. invention
6. retirement
7. treatment
8. prevention
9. settlement
10. management
11. reflection
12. replacement
13. advertisement
14. entertainment
15. arrangement
16. improvement
17. assignment
18. instruction

Page 44
Add It Up!

1. creation
2. civilization
3. judgment
4. confusion
5. starvation
6. competition
7. accompaniment
8. decision
9. permission
10. composition
11. decoration
12. relation
13. separation
14. argument
15. illustration
16. invitation

Morph It!

FILL IN the blanks with the noun version of each verb.

HINT: The answers are all keywords. The suffix "-ion" sometimes morphs into "-tion," "-ition," or "-ation."

Verb	Noun

Example: amaze   amazement

accompany	1. _____
arrange	2. _____
commit	3. _____
compete	4. _____
compose	5. _____
employ	6. _____
excite	7. _____
improve	8. _____
instruct	9. _____
invite	10. _____
produce	11. _____

Alternate Endings

ADD "ion" or "ment" to change the verbs into nouns. FILL IN the blanks with the new words.

Example: pay   payment   subtract   subtraction

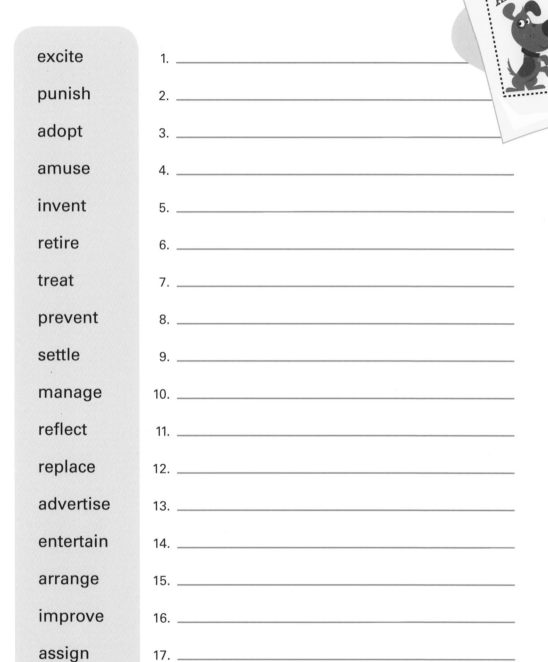

excite	1. _____
punish	2. _____
adopt	3. _____
amuse	4. _____
invent	5. _____
retire	6. _____
treat	7. _____
prevent	8. _____
settle	9. _____
manage	10. _____
reflect	11. _____
replace	12. _____
advertise	13. _____
entertain	14. _____
arrange	15. _____
improve	16. _____
assign	17. _____
instruct	18. _____

Add It Up!

Adding "ion" or "ment" can be tricky. Sometimes you have to drop or add letters to the word before you tack on the endings. Like when *add* becomes *addition*. Or when *divide* becomes *division*.

SOLVE the "problems" by adding the suffix.

HINT: Sometimes you'll add more than "ion" or "ment."

Verb   **Noun**

Example: (divide – de)   +   sion   =   division

(create – e) + ion   1. _____

(civilize – e) + ation   2. _____

(judge – e) + ment   3. _____

(confuse – e) + ion   4. _____

(starve – e) + ation   5. _____

(compete – e) + ition   6. _____

(accompany – y) + iment   7. _____

(decide – de) + sion   8. _____

(permit – t) + ssion   9. _____

(compose – e) + ition   10. _____

(decorate – e) + ion   11. _____

(relate – e) + ion   12. _____

(separate – e) +ion   13. _____

(argue – e) + ment   14. _____

(illustrate – e) + ion   15. _____

(invite – e) + ation   16. _____

Alternate Endings

ADD suffixes to these words to make them into people or other nouns.

HINT: If a verb ends in an "e," drop the "e" before adding the ending. Remember to watch for words that end in -tion, -ition, and -ation.

Verb	Person (+ "-er/-or")	Noun (+ "-ment/-ion")
Example: act	*actor*	*action*

Verb		
compose	1. _____	_____
produce	2. _____	_____
protect	3. _____	_____
settle	4. _____	_____
manage	5. _____	_____
move	6. _____	_____
employ	7. _____	_____
illustrate	8. _____	_____
invent	9. _____	_____
arrange	10. _____	_____

Total Suffixment!

Pick the One!

CIRCLE the correct syllable split for each word.

Example: management   ma•nage•ment   (man•age•ment)

inventor	1. in•vent•or	in•ven•tor
illustration	2. il•lus•tra•tion	ill•us•trat•ion
advertisement	3. ad•ver•tise•ment	ad•vert•ise•ment
composition	4. comp•o•sit•ion	com•po•si•tion
ambition	5. amb•i•tion	am•bi•tion
decoration	6. dec•o•ra•tion	de•co•rat•ion
accompaniment	7. acc•om•pa•nim•ent	ac•com•pa•ni•ment
competition	8. com•pe•ti•tion	comp•et•it•ion
commitment	9. com•mit•ment	comm•i•tment
arrangement	10. ar•range•ment	arr•ang•ement
employment	11. emp•loy•ment	em•ploy•ment
excitement	12. ex•ci•tement	ex•cite•ment
improvement	13. im•prove•ment	imp•ro•vement
instruction	14. inst•ruc•tion	in•struc•tion
invitation	15. in•vi•ta•tion	in•vit•at•ion
production	16. pro•duc•tion	pro•duct•ion

Keywords

You can make adjectives out of verbs, through the magic of the suffix like this:

"-Ive" turns *act* into *active*.

"-Able" turns *break* into *breakable*.

READ the paragraph. The words in **bold** are your keywords.

Arnold is way too **competitive**. We play this **interactive** video game where you need to be really **creative** to win. Arnold's not usually a very **talkative** guy, but whenever I beat him, he starts calling me a cheater. He's so **excitable**! He says it's **unbelievable** that I could ever beat him fairly, even if my win was **decisive**. His anger is **uncontrollable**. After that, he gets **possessive** about the game console (it's his), and won't let me use it. That makes me **uncomfortable**, so I go home. His behavior is **unforgivable** and **inexcusable**!

FILL IN the blanks with the **bold** words in alphabetical order.

1. _____
2. _____
3. _____
4. _____
5. _____
6. _____
7. _____
8. _____
9. _____
10. _____
11. _____
12. _____

Check It!

Page 47

Keywords

1. competitive
2. creative
3. decisive
4. excitable
5. inexcusable
6. interactive
7. possessive
8. talkative
9. unbelievable
10. uncomfortable
11. uncontrollable
12. unforgivable

Page 48

Morph It!

1. believable
2. comfortable
3. competitive
4. controllable
5. creative
6. decisive
7. excitable
8. excusable
9. forgivable
10. interactive
11. possessive
12. talkative

Page 49

Criss Cross

Across
1. excitable
3. unforgivable
4. possessive
5. talkative
7. believable
8. creative

Down
1. excusable
2. controllable
6. decisive

Page 50

Add It Up!

1. effective
2. inventive
3. employable
4. controllable
5. moveable
6. forcible
7. decisive
8. conceivable
9. arguable
10. adorable
11. sensible
12. agreeable
13. decorative
14. reversible
15. explainable
16. forgettable
17. explosive
18. imaginative

Check It!

Morph It!

FILL IN the blanks with keywords to turn each verb into an adjective.

Some of the keywords are missing their "un-" or "in-" prefixes.

Verb	Adjective
	Example: attract attractive / wash washable

believe   1. _____

comfort   2. _____

compete   3. _____

control   4. _____

create   5. _____

decide   6. _____

excite   7. _____

excuse   8. _____

forgive   9. _____

interact   10. _____

possess   11. _____

talk   12. _____

TIP: Sometimes, when a word ends in "e" (like *create*), you have to drop the "e" before adding the suffix. For example, *create*, *creative*. But other times, you keep the "e," like in *moveable*.

Criss Cross

FILL IN the grid by answering the clues.

ACROSS

1. Able to get very excited

3. Not able to be forgiven

4. Likes to possess things

5. Likes to talk a lot

7. Able to be believed

8. Good at creating things

DOWN

1. Able to be excused

2. Able to be controlled

6. Makes decisions easily

Add It Up!

SOLVE the "problems" by adding the suffixes.

Verb	Noun

Example: act + ive = active

effect + ive	1. _____
invent + ive	2. _____
employ + able	3. _____
control + l + able	4. _____
move + able	5. _____
(force – e) + ible	6. _____
(decide – de) + sive	7. _____
(conceive – e) + able	8. _____
(argue – e) + able	9. _____
(adore – e) + able	10. _____
(sense – e) + ible	11. _____
agree + able	12. _____
(decorate – e) + ive	13. _____
(reverse – e) + ible	14. _____
explain + able	15. _____
forget + t + able	16. _____
(explode – de) + sive	17. _____
(imagine – e) + ative	18. _____

Spell Check

READ each sentence. CIRCLE the word that has the wrong suffix.

FILL IN the blanks with those misspelled words. Use the right suffix and spell them right!

Example: My grandma is very (actable) for an old lady. __active__

That stinky spray is pretty effectable at killing bugs.

1. _____

Ashley's curls are uncontrollative when it rains.

2. _____

Is this chair movible, or is it bolted down?

3. _____

This jacket is reversable. Turn it inside out and see!

4. _____

My last karate class was very instructable.

5. _____

Arthur and Veejay are best friends. They're inseparative!

6. _____

Katya's parents are very permittive.

7. _____

That pretty poster on your wall is very decorable.

8. _____

I'll remember our vacation forever. It was unforgettive.

9. _____

Dad's temper is very explodive. He's like a time bomb!

10. _____

Our team won a decidable victory that put us in the playoffs.

11. _____

Sit over here. That lumpy chair isn't very comfortive.

12. _____

Cecilia and Will are dating? That's unbelievible!

13. _____

Marcos and I never fight, because he's very agreeative.

14. _____

Pick the One!

CIRCLE the word in each row with the correct suffix.

Example: act (*active*) *actable*

recognize	1. recognitive	recognizable
submit	2. submissive	submittive
treat	3. treative	treatable
talk	4. talkable	talkative
separate	5. separable	separible
reverse	6. reversable	reversible
force	7. forcive	forcible
create	8. creative	createable
excite	9. excitable	excitive
control	10. controlable	controllable
explode	11. explodive	explosive
hug	12. hugable	huggable
invent	13. inventable	inventive
interact	14. interactive	interactible
effect	15. effective	effectible
decide	16. decidive	decisive
punish	17. punishable	punishive
measure	18. measureable	measurable

Keywords

Here are a couple of suffixes that usually make adjectives.

"-Al" or "-ial" means *about* or *having to do with*, like *bridal*, which means *having to do with the bride.*

"-Ous" or "-ious" means *full of* or *having*, like *joyous*, which means *full of joy.*

READ the paragraph. The words in **bold** are your keywords.

I was very **nervous** at my aunt's wedding. Since I was part of the **bridal** party, I had to walk down the aisle and wear a **formal** dress. Everyone was very **serious** during the ceremony, which included a short **memorial** to Grandma, who died last year. But the party afterward was completely **unceremonious**! People made **humorous** speeches and danced like crazy. My aunt is a very **social** lady with **numerous** friends. Her new husband is a wild, **adventurous**, **musical** guy. (He's in a **famous** band!) They make a great couple.

FILL IN the blanks with the **bold** words in alphabetical order.

1. _____

2. _____

3. _____

4. _____

5. _____

6. _____

7. _____

8. _____

9. _____

10. _____

11. _____

12. _____

✓ Check It!

Page 57

Add It Up!

1. official	9. mysterious
2. spacious	10. survival
3. virtuous	11. colonial
4. beneficial	12. original
5. glorious	13. racial
6. criminal	14. gracious
7. suspicion	15. marvelous
8. personal	16. skeletal

Page 58

Pick the One!

1. adventurous	11. seasonal
2. memorial	12. social
3. digital	13. rental
4. political	14. famous
5. sacrificial	15. natural
6. religious	16. humorous
7. magical	17. glacial
8. universal	18. numerous
9. nervous	19. cultural
10. autumnal	20. alphabetical

Split It!

SPLIT these keywords into syllables, using dots to mark the breaks.

Example: furious   fu•ri•ous

adventurous

bridal

famous

formal

humorous

memorial

musical

nervous

numerous

serious

social

unceremonious

1. _____

2. _____

3. _____

4. _____

5. _____

6. _____

7. _____

8. _____

9. _____

10. _____

11. _____

12. _____

Word Blocks

WRITE the keywords in the blanks. Then FILL IN the word blocks with keywords of the same shape.

Example: Full of fury   furious

Full of nerves   _____

Having to do
with society   _____

Not full of
ceremony   _____

Full of adventure   _____

Having to do
with music   _____

Having to do
with the bride   _____

Full of humor   _____

Full of fame   _____

Spotlight on Suffixes and Roots

Some words with prefixes or suffixes make sense right away, like *musical*. It's easy: music + -al = *musical*. But what about words like *special* or *serious*? "Spec" and "ser" aren't really words—they're word ROOTS. Sometimes the root is a clue to the meaning of a word.

ambitious	annual	enormous	fatal	formal	loyal
moral	funeral	precious	royal	serious	special

FILL IN the blanks with keywords..

1. Dad hates wearing a tuxedo for _____ dinners and dances.

2. Prince William is my favorite member of the _____ family.

3. Team practice is a very _____ occasion. No fooling around!

4. Taj is very _____. He wants to be president some day!

5. I only eat Aunt Bea's cookies once a year, at our _____ picnic.

6. Monster trucks have to be _____ so they can crush little cars.

7. Grandma is a very _____ lady.

   There's no one like her!

8. I can kill a video game alien with one

   _____ shot from my ray gun.

9. Mom and Dad were so sad after their

   friend's _____ .

10. Everyone in our family is a _____ Yankees fan. Go Yanks!

11. Our priest is always talking about _____ stuff, like being honest.

12. Uncle Jim gave his wife a necklace covered with _____ gems.

Add It Up!

SOLVE the "problems" by adding the suffixes.

Example: (fury – y) + ious = furious   (bride – e) + al = bridal

(office – e)	+	ial	1. _____
(space – e)	+	ious	2. _____
(virtue – e)	+	ous	3. _____
(benefit – t)	+	cial	4. _____
(glory – y)	+	ious	5. _____
(crime – e)	+	inal	6. _____
(suspect – ect)	+	icion	7. _____
person	+	al	8. _____
(mystery – y)	+	ious	9. _____
(survive – e)	+	al	10. _____
(colony – y)	+	ial	11. _____
origin	+	al	12. _____
(race – e)	+	ial	13. _____
(grace – e)	+	ious	14. _____
marvel	+	ous	15. _____
(skeleton – on)	+	al	16. _____

Pick the One!

CIRCLE the word in each row with the correct suffix.

Example: *bride* (*bridal*) *brideous*

adventure	1.	adventural	adventurous
memory	2.	memorial	memorous
digit	3.	digital	digitous
politics	4.	politicial	political
sacrifice	5.	sacrificious	sacrificial
religion	6.	religious	religial
magic	7.	magicious	magical
universe	8.	universal	universous
nerves	9.	nervous	nerval
autumn	10.	autumnus	autumnal
season	11.	seasonous	seasonal
society	12.	social	socious
rent	13.	rental	rentious
fame	14.	famous	famial
nature	15.	naturous	natural
humor	16.	humoral	humorous
glacier	17.	glacous	glacial
number	18.	numerous	numberal
culture	19.	cultural	culturous
alphabet	20.	alphabetous	alphabetical

Keywords

Our last suffixes can make verbs out of ordinary nouns like this:

"-Ize" means *to make*, like *capitalize*, which means *to make a capital letter*. "-Ify" also means *to make*, like *beautify*, which means *to make something beautiful*.

READ the paragraph. The words in **bold** are your keywords.

> Yesterday, I helped Uncle Manny **organize** his tools, so he could **simplify** the way he stored them. While we worked, we **socialized** with Jed from next door. I tried to **memorize** all the different tools, but I found one I couldn't **identify**. It **mystified** me. Then I kicked over a jar of nails! Can you **visualize** the floor covered in sharp nails? I was **petrified**, afraid to move. Uncle Manny was **horrified** and **criticized** me angrily. I thought he'd have to be **hospitalized**! I quickly **apologized**, but it took an hour to find all the nails.

FILL IN the blanks with the **bold** words in alphabetical order.

1. _____
2. _____
3. _____
4. _____
5. _____
6. _____
7. _____
8. _____
9. _____
10. _____
11. _____
12. _____

✓ Check It!

Page 59

Keywords

1. apologized
2. criticized
3. horrified
4. hospitalized
5. identify
6. memorize
7. mystified
8. organize
9. petrified
10. simplify
11. socialized
12. visualize

Page 60

Morph it!

1. apologized
2. criticized
3. hospitalized
4. horrified
5. identify
6. memorize
7. mystified
8. simplify
9. socialize
10. visualize

Page 61

Alternate Endings

Verb	+ "-ing"	+ "-ed"
1. apologize	apologizing	apologized
2. hospitalize	hospitalizing	hospitalized
3. mystify	mystifying	mystified
4. memorize	memorizing	memorized
5. simplify	simplifying	simplified
6. visualize	visualizing	visualized
7. socialize	socializing	socialized
8. horrify	horrifying	horrified

Page 62

Add It Up!

1. magnetize
2. purify
3. finalize
4. summarize
5. alphabetize
6. energize
7. familiarize
8. glorify
9. humidify
10. colonize
11. civilize
12. personalize
13. fantasize
14. terrify
15. stabilize
16. justify

Page 63
Spotlight

1. artistic	8. heroic
2. allergic	9. historic
3. athletic	10. idiotic
4. atmospheric	11. magnetic
5. climatic	12. majestic
6. comedic	13. melodic
7. economic	14. poetic

1. fantastic	fantastically
2. energetic	energetically
3. metallic	metallically
4. sympathetic	sympathetically
5. apologetic	apologetically

Page 64
Author! Author!

Check to be sure you used six of the words. Then look them up in a dictionary to see if you used them correctly.

Morph it!

FILL IN the blanks with the keyword verb that matches each noun.

HINT: Use the basic form of the verb with the "-ify" or "-ize" ending.

Example: beauty   beautify

apology   1. _____

critic   2. _____

hospital   3. _____

horror   4. _____

identity   5. _____

memory   6. _____

mystery   7. _____

simple   8. _____

social   9. _____

visual   10. _____

Alternate Endings

FILL IN the blanks with basic forms of the keywords. Then ADD the verb endings to make the different verb forms.

HINT: See the example for how to treat verbs that end in "y."

Example: Make beautiful   beautify   beautifying   beautified

Verb	Verb + "-ing"	Verb + "-ed"
Make an apology		
1. _____	_____	_____
Put in the hospital		
2. _____	_____	_____
Make a mystery		
3. _____	_____	_____
Put in your memory		
4. _____	_____	_____
Make more simple		
5. _____	_____	_____
Make visual		
6. _____	_____	_____
Be social		
7. _____	_____	_____
Make someone feel horror		
8. _____	_____	_____

Add It Up!

SOLVE the "problems" by adding the suffixes.

Example: (fury – y) + ious   = furious

magnet	+	ize	1. _____
(pure – e)	+	ify	2. _____
final	+	ize	3. _____
(summary – y)	+	ize	4. _____
alphabet	+	ize	5. _____
(energy – y)	+	ize	6. _____
familiar	+	ize	7. _____
(glory – y)	+	ify	8. _____
humid	+	ify	9. _____
(colony – y)	+	ize	10. _____
civil	+	ize	11. _____
personal	+	ize	12. _____
(fantasy – y)	+	ize	13. _____
(terror – or)	+	ify	14. _____
(stable – le)	+	ilize	15. _____
just	+	ify	16. _____

Spotlight on Just Add "-ic"

Suffixes are terrific! How about one more? When you add "-ic" to a verb like *terrify*, or to a noun like *angel*, voila! You get the adjectives *terrific* and *angelic*. Try it out!

ADD "-ic" to the words to turn them into adjectives.

HINT: If a word ends in an "e" or a "y," drop it!

Example: magnet   magnetic

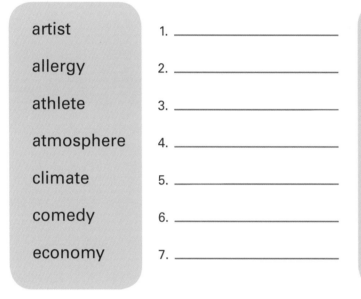

artist	1. _____	hero	8. _____
allergy	2. _____	history	9. _____
athlete	3. _____	idiot	10. _____
atmosphere	4. _____	magnet	11. _____
climate	5. _____	majesty	12. _____
comedy	6. _____	melody	13. _____
economy	7. _____	poet	14. _____

Here are some tricky ones! Make these into both adjectives and adverbs.

HINT: To make an adverb from an adjective, just add a double suffix "-al" + "-ly" = "-ally."

	Adjective	**Adverb**
Example: drama + tic =	*dramatic*	*dramatically*

(fantasy – y) + tic	1. _____	_____
(energy – y) + etic	2. _____	_____
metal + lic	3. _____	_____
(sympathy – y) + etic	4. _____	_____
(apology – y) + etic	5. _____	_____

The Last Suffixes

Author! Author!

It's your turn to do the writing. Use at least six of the words to write a story, a poem, or a list of crazy sentences. Have fun!

angelic	horrify	disagreeable	amusement
entertainer	uncontrollable	magnetic	unforgettable
flawless	apologize	invitation	interruption

Blank Out!

LOOK AT the clue. Then WRITE the matching suffix in each blank.

-y	-ful	-less	-ness	-er	-or	-ly	-ment
-ion	-ive	-able	-al	-ous	-ify	-ize	-ic

Means *full of*:

Means *lacking*:

Makes a verb:

Makes a verb into a noun:

Makes an adverb:

Makes a verb into a person:

Makes an adjective into a noun:

Makes a noun into an adjective:

Makes a verb into an adjective:

1. care___ ___ ___

2. care___ ___ ___ ___

3. simpl___ ___ ___

4. magnet___ ___ ___

5. commit___ ___ ___ ___

6. protect___ ___ ___

7. quick___ ___

8. instruct___ ___

9. teach___ ___

10. sweet___ ___ ___ ___

11. smell___

12. music___ ___

13. magnet___ ___

14. humor___ ___ ___

15. wash___ ___ ___ ___

16. possess___ ___ ___

Check It!

Page 65
Blank Out!

1. careful	9. teacher
2. careless	10. sweetness
3. simplify	11. smelly
4. magnetize	12. musical
5. commitment	13. magnetic
6. protection	14. humorous
7. quickly	15. washable
8. instructor	16. possessive

Page 66
Pick the One!

1. reminder	10. preachy
2. simply	11. critical
3. permissive	12. promptly
4. adeptness	13. professor
5. central	14. constantly
6. horrific	15. penniless
7. purify	16. illustrator
8. offensive	17. location
9. sincerely	18. forgetfulness

Page 67
Morph It!

1. colonial
2. apologize, apologetically
3. criticize, critically
4. mystify, mysterious, mysteriously
5. energize, energetic, energetically
6. personalize, personally
7. magnetize, magnetic, magnetically
8. civilization, civilize, civilly
9. fantasize, fantastic
10. horrify, horrific, horrifically
11. instruction, instructively
12. agreeable, agreeably
13. excite, excitable, excitably
14. believer, believable, believably

Page 68
Word Search

F	E	O	V	E	R	C	O	O	K	E	D
U	M	L	E	S	I	W	V	G	K	U	I
N	P	Y	J	O	Y	F	U	L	U	N	S
D	O	U	B	T	L	E	S	S	N	T	A
E	W	U	W	L	O	B	L	E	S	A	B
R	E	N	D	E	A	N	T	I	U	N	L
W	R	D	I	S	C	O	U	R	A	G	E
E	N	O	S	H	A	R	M	F	U	L	U
I	U	N	S	X	Q	P	P	L	Y	E	N
G	Y	E	F	A	I	T	H	L	E	S	S
H	D	I	S	X	W	E	R	F	U	L	L
T	A	S	T	E	L	E	S	S	I	M	T

Pick the One!

CIRCLE the word with the correct suffix.

Example: Someone who acts is an   *(actor)*   *action*

Something that reminds you is a	1. reminder	remindment
To be simple, you do it	2. simply	simplely
If you permit things, you are	3. permittive	permissive
An adept person is known for	4. adeptment	adeptness
If it's in the center, it is	5. central	centrous
Something that horrifies you is	6. horrifious	horrific
To make something pure, you	7. purify	purifize
When you offend, you're being	8. offensive	offendify
To be sincere, you do it	9. sincerely	sincerious
If you preach a lot, you are	10. preachify	preachy
If you like to criticize, you are	11. critical	critious
To be prompt, you do it	12. promptious	promptly
Someone who professes is a	13. professor	professicator
To be constant, you do things	14. constantize	constantly
No pennies? Then you're	15. penniless	penniful
If you illustrate, then you're an	16. illustral	illustrator
You are located at your	17. location	locatement
A forgetful person suffers from	18. forgetion	forgetfulness

Morph It!

FILL IN the blanks by writing the correct form of the word.

	Noun	Verb	Adjective	Adverb
1.	colony	colonize	_____	colonially
2.	apology	_____	apologetic	_____
3.	critic	_____	critical	_____
4.	mystery	_____	_____	_____
5.	energy	_____	_____	_____
6.	person	_____	personal	_____
7.	magnet	_____	_____	_____
8.	_____	_____	civil	_____
9.	fantasy	_____	_____	fantastically
10.	horror	_____	_____	_____
11.	_____	instruct	instructive	_____
12.	agreement	agree	_____	_____
13.	excitement	_____	_____	_____
14.	_____	believe	_____	_____

Word Search

CHANGE the prefix or suffix to make the opposite of the words listed. FILL IN the blanks with the new words. Then CIRCLE the words in the word grid. Words go down and across, not diagonally or backwards.

overweight _____

tasteful _____

encourage _____

entangle _____

undercooked _____

overpower _____

enable _____

harmless _____

doubtful _____

faithful _____

joyless _____

F	E	O	V	E	R	C	O	O	K	E	D
U	M	L	E	S	I	W	V	G	K	U	I
N	P	Y	J	O	Y	F	U	L	U	N	S
D	O	U	B	T	L	E	S	S	N	T	A
E	W	U	W	L	O	B	L	E	S	A	B
R	E	N	D	E	A	N	T	I	U	N	L
W	R	D	I	S	C	O	U	R	A	G	E
E	N	O	S	H	A	R	M	F	U	L	U
I	U	N	S	X	Q	P	P	L	Y	E	N
G	Y	E	F	A	I	T	H	L	E	S	S
H	D	I	S	X	W	E	R	F	U	L	L
T	A	S	T	E	L	E	S	S	I	M	T

Keywords

When you have to spell a word you don't know, try to figure out its ROOT. What's a root? It's what's left when you take off the prefixes and suffixes.

Try these out:
Equalize comes from the root "equa" (also "equi") which means *equal*.
Scribble comes from the root "scrib" (also "script") which means *write*.

READ the paragraph. The words in **bold** are your keywords.

Hollywood, here I come! I **subscribe** to many movie magazines and **transcribe** scenes from my favorite films so I can practice them. My friend Sammy **describes** me as "a future movie star." He even asked me to **scribble** an **inscription** in his autograph album! He **equates** me with the star of his favorite TV show, and says I am **equally** talented. All I need is the right **script**! Mom thinks acting is **equivalent** to joining the circus and says I should go to the doctor and get a **prescription** for anti-Hollywood pills. Ha ha! Whether I'm singing or solving **equations** for math class, my talent shines all the way to the **equator**!

FILL IN the blanks with the **bold** words in alphabetical order.

1. _____
2. _____
3. _____
4. _____
5. _____
6. _____

7. _____
8. _____
9. _____
10. _____
11. _____
12. _____

✓ Check It!

Page 69
Keywords

1. describes
2. equally
3. equates
4. equations
5. equator
6. equivalent
7. inscription
8. prescription
9. scribble
10. script
11. subscribe
12. transcribe

Page 70
Stack Up

"Equi/Equa" Root
1. equal
2. equates
3. equations
4. equator
5. equivalent

"Script/Scrib" Root
1. describes
2. inscription
3. prescription
4. scribble
5. script
6. subscribe
7. transcribe

Page 71
Criss Cross

Across
3. prescription
6. equivalent
7. script
8. equations

Down
1. describes
2. transcribe
4. inscription
5. equator

Page 72
Word Blocks

sub(scrip)tion
pre(scrib)ed
(equi)distant
tran(scrip)tions
in(equa)lity
(equa)lize
(equi)nox

1. transcriptions
2. equinox
3. inequality
4. equidistant
5. subscription
6. prescribed
7. equalize

Stack Up

SORT the keywords by their roots.

describes	equal	equates	equations
equator	equivalent	inscription	prescription
scribble	script	subscribe	transcribe

Check It!

Page 73

Split It!

1. de•scribe
2. e•qual•ize
3. eq•ui•ta•ble
4. e•qua•tion
5. e•qua•tor
6. e•qua•to•ri•al
7. e•qui•dis•tant
8. e•qui•nox
9. e•quiv•a•lent
10. in•scrip•tion
11. pre•scrip•tion
12. scrib•ble
13. sub•scribe
14. tran•scribe

Page 74

Morph It!

1. equalize, equally
2. equation, equitable
3. description
4. inscribe, inscribable
5. prescription, prescribable
6. subscription, subscribable
7. transcribe, transcribable

1. inequality
2. indescribable
3. unequal
4. resubscribe

"Equi/Equa" Root
Example: equinox

1. _____

2. _____

3. _____

4. _____

5. _____

"Script/Scrib" Root
Example: unscripted

1. _____

2. _____

3. _____

4. _____

5. _____

6. _____

7. _____

Criss Cross

FILL IN the grid by answering the clues with keywords.

ACROSS

3. A written note from a doctor to the pharmacist

6. A longer way of saying equal

7. The written text of a play or movie

8. Math statements with equal signs

DOWN

1. Tells or writes how something looks

2. To write something down, or copy it

4. A written message in or on something

5. A line that divides the world into two equal halves

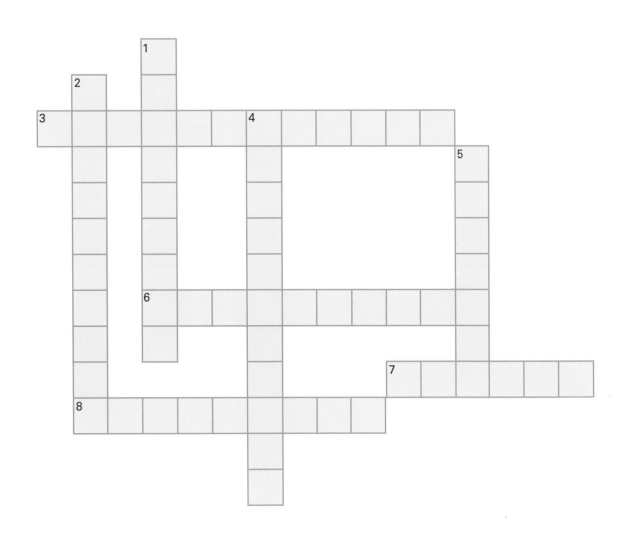

Word Blocks

CIRCLE the root "equi/equa" or "scrip/scrib" in each sentence. Then FILL IN the word blocks with the words of the same shape.

HINT: Use the whole word, not just the root!

For her birthday, I gave Mom a subscription to a gardening magazine.

When I had the flu, my doctor prescribed some antibiotics.

My house is equidistant from two comic book stores.

To practice typing, I make transcriptions of my favorite fairy tales.

There is serious inequality at camp, where the girls get the nicest cabins.

My brother gets a bigger allowance, so I asked Mom to equalize our allowances.

Day and night are the same length on the day of the equinox.

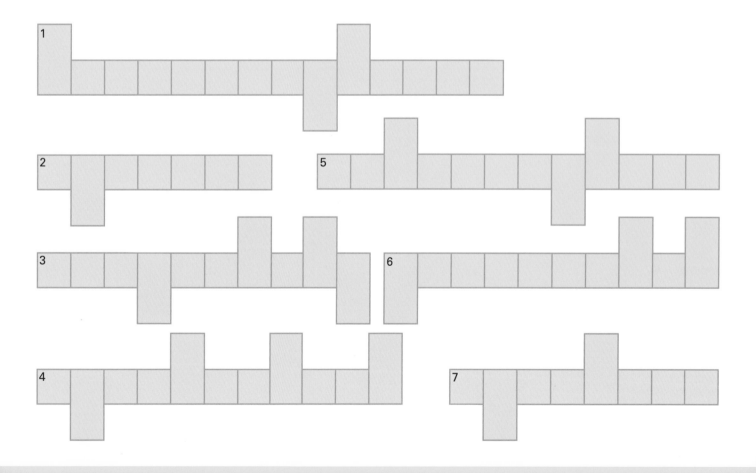

Split It!

SPLIT these words into syllables, using dots to mark the breaks.

HINT: Don't forget that syllables with short vowels usually end in a consonant.

Example: equal   e•qual

describe	1. _____
equalize	2. _____
equitable	3. _____
equation	4. _____
equator	5. _____
equatorial	6. _____
equidistant	7. _____
equinox	8. _____
equivalent	9. _____
inscription	10. _____
prescription	11. _____
scribble	12. _____
subscribe	13. _____
transcribe	14. _____

Morph It!

FILL IN the blanks by writing the correct form of the word.

	Noun	Verb	Adjective	Adverb
1.	equality	_____	equal	_____
2.	_____	equate	_____	equitably
3.	_____	describe	describable	
4.	inscription	_____	_____	
5.	_____	prescribe	_____	
6.	_____	subscribe	_____	
7.	transcription	_____	_____	

Now FILL IN these blanks to complete each word with one of the words above.

1. There is so much in_____ at karate! Girls get treated differently!

2. I don't know what to say. Mrs. Simpson's hair is in_____!

3. Seriously, the lunch lady gives out un_____ portions.

4. I sent in my form to re_____ to my rock collecting magazine.

Keywords

Even though *equal* and *scribe* can stand alone, roots don't usually work by themselves. They need help from prefixes and suffixes. Here are some roots that can't stand alone.

Manually comes from the root "man," which means *hand*.
Corpse comes from the root "corp," which means *body*.
Captain comes from the root "cap," which means *head*.
Capture comes from another root, "cap," which means *to take*.

READ the paragraph. The words in **bold** are your keywords.

On my favorite TV show last night, the cops found a **corpse** inside a **manicure** shop (and it wasn't getting its nails done!)! I guessed right away that the killer was the head of a big **corporation** that **manufactured** robots. I could tell the guy was guilty by his suspicious **manner**. He **demanded** a lawyer, then **managed** to **manipulate** the police into letting him go. The bad guy left the country in a boat. Luckily, the boat **capsized**, and the police **captain commanded** his men to **capture** the criminal.

FILL IN the blanks with the **bold** words in alphabetical order.

1. _____
2. _____
3. _____
4. _____
5. _____
6. _____
7. _____
8. _____
9. _____
10. _____
11. _____
12. _____

✓ Check It!

Page 79
Morph It!

1. commander, command
2. management, manager, manage
3. manipulation, manipulate
4. incorporate
5. capitalize
6. captor, capture, captive
7. captivate

1. manipulative   4. manager
2. commanding   5. captivity
3. captivate   6. capital

Page 80
Pick the One!

1. cap•i•tal•ize   9. man•i•cure
2. ca•pri•cious   10. ma•nip•u•late
3. cap•sized   11. man•ners
4. cap•ti•vate   12. man•u•fac•ture
5. in•cor•po•rat•ed   13. man•u•script
6. cor•po•ral   14. man•u•al•ly
7. cor•pu•lent   15. com•mand•ment
8. man•age•ment   16. de•mand•ing

Stack Up

SORT the keywords by their roots. FILL IN the blanks with the sorted words.

capsized	captain	capture	commanded
corporation	corpse	demanded	managed
manicure	manipulate	manner	manufactured

"Man" Root
Example: manuscript

1. _____
2. _____
3. _____
4. _____
5. _____
6. _____
7. _____

"Corp" Root
Example: corps

1. _____
2. _____

"Cap" Root
Example: captor

1. _____
2. _____
3. _____

Word Search

FILL IN the blanks with forms of the keywords. Then CIRCLE the words in the word grid. Words go down and across, not diagonally or backwards.

1. John rocked the boat to make it _____ and dump us out.

2. Luke was walking and talking in a strange _____ at the mall today.

3. When I'm sick, I always _____ Mom to make me chicken soup.

4. Hendrick can _____ Lee into doing anything!

5. The team _____ is the one who sets the line-up.

6. My sister always _____ the biggest slice of pie. What a brat!

7. Ew! Your fingernails are a mess. Time to get a _____.

8. Will Lucy ever _____ to get to practice on time?

9. My aunt's company _____ MP3 players. Cool, huh?

10. Aunt June runs a nonprofit _____ that sends medicine to Africa.

C	O	M	M	A	N	D	C	O	R	P	D	E
O	C	A	P	T	A	I	N	X	E	D	Y	W
M	A	N	U	F	A	C	T	U	R	E	S	M
A	P	I	C	V	Q	P	C	A	P	K	T	A
N	S	C	O	R	P	O	R	A	T	I	O	N
N	I	U	R	M	D	E	M	A	N	D	S	A
E	Z	R	P	U	O	O	A	B	M	A	N	G
R	E	E	M	A	N	I	P	U	L	A	T	E

Word Blocks

FILL IN the root "man," "corp," or "cap" in each sentence. Then FILL IN the word blocks with words of the same shape.

HINT: Use the whole word, not just the root.

Fern is so _____ricious! You never know what she'll do next.

Can you open the door _____ually if the electricity goes out?

In the story, a princess was kidnapped. Her _____tor was a smelly pirate.

All the important lawmakers hang out at the _____itol building.

That squirrel is so fat! He's totally _____pulent.

Maybe if you don't _____italize all the letters, it'll be easier to read.

"Let me go, you smelly pirate!" cried the _____tive princess.

Dad's book is just a _____uscript. It hasn't been published yet.

Morph It!

FILL IN the blanks by writing the correct form of the word.

Noun	Person	Verb	Adjective
1. commandment	_____	_____	commanding
2. _____	_____	_____	managerial
3. _____	manipulator	_____	manipulative
4. corporation		_____	incorporated
5. capital	capitalist	_____	capital
6. captivity	_____	_____	_____
7. captivation	captivator	_____	captivating

Now FILL IN these blanks with one of the words above.

1. It's very _____ to offer me candy if I'll do what you want.

2. You have to use a _____ voice when you train your dog.

3. Cartoons totally _____ my little brother. You can't tear him away!

4. My sister was promoted to _____ of the restaurant.

5. My mom doesn't believe that wild animals should be kept in _____.

6. Beebee doesn't like to use any _____ letters in her e-mails.

More about Roots

Pick the One!

CIRCLE the correct syllable split for each word.

HINT: Listen to the vowel sounds. You may have to split the root.

Example: demand (de•mand) *dem•and*

1. capitalize   cap•i•tal•ize   ca•pi•ta•lize

2. capricious   ca•pri•cious   cap•ric•ious

3. capsized   ca•psiz•ed   cap•sized

4. captivate   cap•ti•vate   cap•tiv•ate

5. incorporated   in•corp•or•at•ed   in•cor•po•rat•ed

6. corporal   cor•po•ral   corp•o•ral

7. corpulent   cor•pu•lent   corp•u•lent

8. management   man•ag•ement   man•age•ment

9. manicure   man•ic•ure   man•i•cure

10. manipulate   man•i•pu•late   ma•nip•u•late

11. manners   man•ners   mann•ers

12. manufacture   ma•nu•fact•ure   man•u•fac•ture

13. manuscript   man•u•script   ma•nu•script

14. manually   man•u•al•ly   ma•nu•all•y

15. commandment   comm•and•ment   com•mand•ment

16. demanding   de•mand•ing   dem•and•ing

Keywords

Here are some more roots that can't live on their own:

Dictate comes from the root "dict" (also "dic"), which means *to say*.
Conductor comes from the root "duct" (also "duc"), which means *to lead or take*.
Convert comes from the root "vert" (also "vers"), which means *to turn*.

READ the paragraph. The words in **bold** are your keywords.

> If you look up the word *dictator* in the **dictionary**, you'll see a picture of my gymnastics coach. She **conducts** every training session like she's an army general. No **conversation** allowed! Once she **reduced** Karina to tears because her handstand wasn't perfectly **vertical**. When she **introduced** a new kid and he corrected the way she pronounced his name, she yelled at him for **contradicting** her. After we **educated** our parents about her true nature, our coach **reversed** her behavior for a while. But I **predict** she will soon **revert** to her old ways!

FILL IN the blanks with the **bold** words in alphabetical order.

1. _____

2. _____

3. _____

4. _____

5. _____

6. _____

7. _____

8. _____

9. _____

10. _____

11. _____

12. _____

Stack Up

SORT the keywords by their roots.

conducts	contradicting	conversation	dictator
dictionary	educated	introduced	predict
reduced	revert	reversed	vertical

"Dic/Dict" Root
Example: verdict

1. _____

2. _____

3. _____

4. _____

"Duc/Duct" Root
Example: produce

1. _____

2. _____

3. _____

4. _____

"Vert/Vers" Root
Example: convert

1. _____

2. _____

3. _____

4. _____

Criss Cross

FILL IN the grid by answering the clues with forms of the keywords.

ACROSS

1. A place where you can look up words

4. To lead a class, meeting, or musical group

5. To turn back, go the opposite way

7. To say or guess something before it happens

8. To argue or say the opposite thing

DOWN

1. Someone who tells everyone what to do

2. The act of taking turns talking

3. To make smaller

6. To lead someone toward knowledge

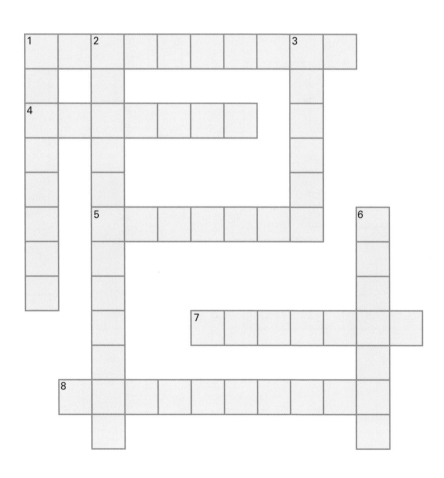

Word Blocks

WRITE the root "dic/dict," "duc/duct," or "vert/vers" in each sentence. Then FILL IN the word blocks with the words of the same shape.

There's a lot of di_____ity in our neighborhood. We're very multiracial.

I'm repro_____ing a famous painting for art class.

Shama answered an ad_____tisement in the paper for a babysitting job.

I love when we drive in the con_____tible with the top down!

The new pool at our YMCA is de_____ated to a kid who died of cancer.

Leonard works on his _____tion in speech class.

Did you hear that the Scoop Shop is intro_____ing a new flavor?

I wonder how many planets are in the uni_____se?

Morph It!

FILL IN the blanks with the correct form of the word.

HINT: All but one of the nouns ends in "ion."

Noun	Verb
1. _____	advertise
2. contradiction	_____
3. _____	converse
4. conversion	_____
5. _____	dedicate
6. _____	deduce
7. dictation	_____
8. _____	divert
9. _____	educate
10. introduction	_____
11. _____	produce
12. _____	reduce

Now FILL IN these blanks with one of the words above.

1. Good detectives are masters of _____.

2. From the mud on your clothes, I _____ you've been outside.

3. Use a photocopier to _____ that newspaper article.

4. My dad has to _____ letters for his assistant to type up.

5. You have to _____ your dollars to pounds when you go to England.

6. Engineers build dams to _____ rivers from their natural course.

Split It!

SPLIT these words into syllables, using dots to mark the breaks.

Example: produce   pro•duce

advertise

vertical

dictator

dictionary

introduction

deduction

reproduction

production

education

reversal

conversion

conversation

universe

diversify

indication

dedication

1. _____

2. _____

3. _____

4. _____

5. _____

6. _____

7. _____

8. _____

9. _____

10. _____

11. _____

12. _____

13. _____

14. _____

15. _____

16. _____

Keywords

Once you know how to spell one word using the root, you should be able to spell most of the words that share the same root. Here are three more roots:

Finish comes from the root "fin," which means *end*.
Avenue comes from the root "ven," which means *come*.
Mission comes from the root "mis" (also "mit"), which means *send*.

READ the paragraph. The words in **bold** are your keywords.

> Nothing can **prevent** me from going to the sci-fi **convention**! Last year, I didn't get **permission** to go. So I made a **commitment** to my parents that I would **finish** my homework every night and **submit** to any other chores or commands that they could **invent** for me to do. It **definitely** worked! I now hold in my hands a ticket that says "**admit** one." This will be quite an **adventure**! The grand **finale** will be a special screening of the **final** episode of *Space 2169*, my favorite show. I can't wait!

FILL IN the blanks with the **bold** words in alphabetical order.

1. _____
2. _____
3. _____
4. _____
5. _____
6. _____

7. _____
8. _____
9. _____
10. _____
11. _____
12. _____

✓ Check It!

Page 87

Keywords

1. admit	7. finale
2. adventure	8. finish
3. commitment	9. invent
4. convention	10. permission
5. definitely	11. prevent
6. final	12. submit

Page 88

Stack Up

"Fin" Root	"Ven" Root
1. definitely	1. adventure
2. final	2. convention
3. finale	3. invent
4. finish	4. prevent

"Mit/Mis" Root
1. admit
2. commitment
3. permission
4. submit

Page 89

Word Search

```
C O M M P R E M I T
C O N V E N T I O N
W M I T R L B N P F
F V A D M I T V R I
I F I N I S H E E N
N M I S S V F N V X
A F I N S P K T E R
L D E F I N E Q N V
E W E C O M M I T E
A D V E N T U R E N
```

Page 90

Morph It!

1. invent, inventive
2. prevention, preventively
3. permission, permissive
4. submit, submissively
5. define, definite
6. commit
7. convention
8. admit

1. admission	4. inventive
2. submit	5. definite
3. commitment	6. convene

✓ **Check It!**

Page 91

Spotlight on "Nat"

Long "A" Sound	Short "A" Sound
1. na•tion	1. na•tion•al
2. na•tive	2. nat•u•ral
3. na•ture	3. su•per•nat•u•ral
4. pre•na•tal	4. mul•ti•na•tion•al
5. in•nate	

Page 92

Author! Author!

Check to be sure you used six of the words. Then look them up in a dictionary to see if you used them correctly.

Stack Up

SORT the keywords by their roots.

admit	adventure	commitment	convention
definitely	final	finale	finish
invent	permission	prevent	submit

"Fin" Root
Example: finalist

1. _____

2. _____

3. _____

4. _____

"Ven" Root
Example: convenient

1. _____

2. _____

3. _____

4. _____

"Mis/Mit" Root
Example: transmit

1. _____

2. _____

3. _____

4. _____

Word Search

FILL IN the blanks with keywords. Then CIRCLE the words in the word grid. Words go down and across, not diagonally or backwards.

1. Luis has the flu, which will _____ him from going to the picnic.

2. Sheryl likes to read _____ stories, where kids travel and face danger.

3. Someday, I'm going to _____ a car that drives itself.

4. The magician's _____ was to cut a girl in half and make her disappear.

5. You can't go on the trip without your parent's _____.

6. The usher won't _____ you without a ticket.

7. Dad has to go to a _____ of computer programmers. Boring!

8. Serena needs more time so she can _____ her sculpture.

C	O	M	M	P	R	E	M	I	T
C	O	N	V	E	N	T	I	O	N
W	M	I	T	R	L	B	N	P	F
F	V	A	D	M	I	T	V	R	I
I	F	I	N	I	S	H	E	E	N
N	M	I	S	S	V	F	N	V	X
A	F	I	N	S	P	K	T	E	R
L	D	E	F	I	N	E	Q	N	V
E	W	E	C	O	M	M	I	T	E
A	D	V	E	N	T	U	R	E	N

Bonus

There are two words that contain the same root as two keywords. Can you find them?

Morph It!

FILL IN the blanks by writing the correct form of the word.

	Noun	Verb	Adjective	Adverb
1.	invention	_____	_____	inventively
2.	_____	prevent	preventive	_____
3.	_____	permit	_____	permissively
4.	submission	_____	submissive	_____
5.	definition	_____	_____	definitely
6.	commitment	_____		
7.	_____	convene		
8.	admission	_____		

Now FILL IN these blanks with one of the words above.

1. For this show, the price of _____ is ten dollars.

2. Did you _____ your information form online?

3. By coming to practice, you show your _____ to the team.

4. Clara found an _____ way to fix her glasses with a paper clip.

5. We finally sold the house, so our move is now _____.

6. My Dad will _____ all of us when we have a family meeting.

Spotlight on "Nat"

"Nat" means *born*, so a *native* is someone born here. But there's more to "nat" than meets the eye. Say these two words out loud: *natural* and *nature*. The first syllables sound different, right? Let's take a closer look, using these keywords:

SORT these words, and SPLIT them into syllables, using dots to mark the breaks.

nation	national	native	natural	nature
prenatal	supernatural	multinational	innate	

Long "A" Sound	**Short "A" Sound**
Example: ba•by	*Example: bab•ble*
1. _____	1. _____
2. _____	2. _____
3. _____	3. _____
4. _____	4. _____
5. _____	

Author! Author!

It's your turn to do the writing. Use at least six of these words to write a story, a poem, or a list of crazy sentences. Have fun!

equalize	scribble	subscribe	manicure	demand	corpse
corpulent	captive	dictator	introduce	reduce	advertise

Stack Up

SORT the words by their roots.

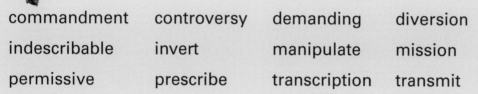

commandment	controversy	demanding	diversion
indescribable	invert	manipulate	mission
permissive	prescribe	transcription	transmit

"Script/Scrib" Root (To Write)
Example: scribble

1. _____

2. _____

3. _____

"Man" Root (Hand)
Example: scribble

1. _____

2. _____

3. _____

"Vert" Root (To Turn)
Example: convert

1. _____

2. _____

3. _____

"Mit" Root (To Send)
Example: admission

1. _____

2. _____

3. _____

✓ Check It!

Page 93
Stack Up

"Script/Scrib" Root
1. indescribable
2. prescribe
3. transcription

"Man" Root
1. commandment
2. demanding
3. manipulate

"Vert" Root
1. controversy
2. diversion
3. invert

"Mit" Root
1. mission
2. permissive
3. transmit

Page 94
Criss Cross

Across
2. indescribable
4. commandment
6. controversy
7. invert
8. mission

Down
1. permissive
3. demanding
5. diversion

Page 95
Pick the One!

1. prediction
2. revert
3. finale
4. equinox
5. manuscript
6. capture
7. dictator
8. reproduce
9. conductor
10. prevent
11. vertical
12. prenatal
13. transmit
14. infinite
15. equilateral
16. corpulent
17. manage

Page 96
Morph It!

1. capital, capital
2. captivation, captivate, captivatingly
3. commandment, command, commandingly
4. conversation, converse, conversational
5. definition, definite, definitely
6. education, educate, educationally
7. equality, equally
8. equitable
9. invention, inventively
10. management, manage, managerial

Criss Cross

FILL IN the grid by answering the clues.

HINT: Don't forget to use a dictionary if you need help!

ACROSS

2. You just can't even say how it was!

4. An order you must obey

6. An argument over an opinion

7. To turn something upside-down

8. A job or task you are sent to do

DOWN

1. Really easygoing, allowing a lot

3. Constantly asking for things

5. It turns you away from your course

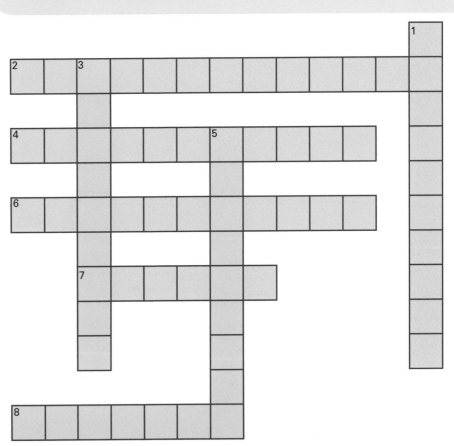

Pick the One!

CIRCLE the correct answer to each clue.

Example: Someone who teaches is an (educator) *edictator*

1. When you say something beforehand prescription prediction
2. To turn back to the way you were revert reduce
3. The last act of a show is the finale capital
4. When day and night are the same length corpinox equinox
5. Something you write by hand interscript manuscript
6. To take someone away capture captive
7. Someone who tells everybody what to do ductator dictator
8. To make a copy produce reproduce
9. If you lead the band, you are the conductor conducter
10. Stop something from happening prevent prescribe
11. Turned straight up and down corporal vertical
12. Before birth prenatural prenatal
13. To send something across space transmit transduce
14. With no ending incapable infinite
15. Having equal sides multilateral equilateral
16. Very fat capulent corpulent
17. To take things into your own hands manage convene

Morph It!

FILL IN the blanks by writing the correct form of the word.

	Noun	Verb	Adjective	Adverb
1.		capitalize		capitally
2.			captivating	
3.			commanding	
4.				conversationally
5.		define		
6.			educational	
7.		equalize	equal	
8.	equation	equate		equitably
9.		invent	inventive	
10.				managerially

Keywords

Some words sound the same but are spelled differently. These words are called HOMOPHONES. Sometimes, two words sound the same because they have similar (but not identical) prefixes or suffixes.

READ the paragraph. The words in **bold** are your keywords.

In the movie *Castle Crash*, the hero is all set to marry a princess, **except** her family won't **accept** him. Have you **seen** it? The best **scene** is when he has to hide in a basement, standing up to his **waist** in disgusting sewer **waste** and sludge. But all that muck doesn't **lessen** our hero's courage! He plans to teach the royal family a **lesson**. He sneaks in while **they're** asleep in **their** rooms. But the family has a **guest** (an old lady), and she's **guessed** his plan. I won't tell you how it ends. But it's so exciting!

FILL IN the blanks with the **bold** words in alphabetical order.

1. _____
2. _____
3. _____
4. _____
5. _____
6. _____
7. _____
8. _____
9. _____
10. _____
11. _____
12. _____

✓ Check It!

Page 97
Keywords

1. accept
2. except
3. guessed
4. guest
5. lessen
6. lesson
7. scene
8. seen
9. their
10. they're
11. waist
12. waste

Page 98
Blank Out!

1. scene
2. guest
3. except
4. lessen
5. waist
6. they're
7. waste
8. their
9. seen
10. lesson

Page 99
Criss Cross

ACROSS
1. guessed
4. lessen
6. except
7. they're

DOWN
1. guest
2. scene
3. waist
5. accept

Page 100
Blank Out!

1. billed, build
2. allowed, aloud
3. Capitol, capital
4. close, clothes
5. flu, flew
6. medal, metal
7. pairs, pears
8. to, too
9. seen, scene
10. wheel, we'll
11. overdue, overdo
12. there, their
13. You're, your
14. Colonel, kernel
15. band, banned
16. wait, weight
17. sense, cents

✓ **Check It!**

Page 101

Spell Check

1. chews	9. too
2. banned	10. world
3. overseas	11. guest
4. peak	12. sense
5. colonel	13. praise
6. principal	14. lessen
7. weight	15. They're
8. waste	16. guilt

Page 102

Spotlight on Homographs

1. i	9. l
2. k	10. n
3. o	11. b
4. a	12. e
5. f	13. p
6. c	14. d
7. m	15. g
8. j	16. h

Blank Out!

FILL IN the blanks with the correct keyword to finish the sentence.

1. My little sister always cries and makes a _____ when she doesn't get her way.

2. Lorna was mean to every _____ at her party.

3. I like everything about Raoul _____ his bad breath.

4. Mom gave me an aspirin to _____ the pain after I banged my head.

5. That outfit would look better with a belt around your _____.

6. My parents are so weird. Today, _____ wearing matching jackets!

7. My pal Duncan says talking to girls is a _____ of time.

8. The twins are hungry. Are _____ bottles ready?

9. I can't find my sunglasses. Have you _____ them?

12. Fiona has to go to her piano _____ right after lunch.

Criss Cross

FILL IN the grid by answering the clues with keywords.

ACROSS

1. Figured out, or tried to

4. To make less

6. A word you use to leave something out

7. A contraction

DOWN

1. Someone who goes to a party

2. A section of a show or a play

3. About halfway between your neck and your knees

5. Welcome or receive

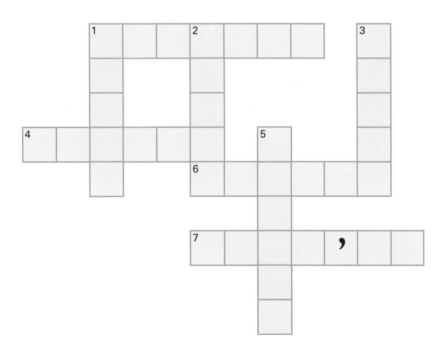

Homophones

Blank Out!

FILL IN the blanks with the correct word to finish the sentence.

Example: threw/through: Arnold <u>threw</u> the ball <u>through</u> the hoop.

billed/build: 1. The carpenter _____ my parents $100 to _____ the shelves.

aloud/allowed: 2. No one's _____ to read _____ at the library.

Capitol/capital: 3. The _____ building is spelled with a _____ letter "c."

close/clothes: 4. I'm very _____ to filling my closet with new _____.

flew/flu: 5. When Mom got the _____, we _____ home from Florida early.

medal/metal: 6. My swimming _____ is made of shiny gold _____.

pears/pairs: 7. We're painting _____ of _____ for art class.

too/to: 8. Ingrid is going _____ sled with us _____!

seen/scene: 9. Have you _____ the _____ with Homer and the bear?

we'll/wheel: 10. You take the _____ and _____ push the car.

overdue/overdo: 11. I know your project is _____, but don't _____ it!

there/their: 12. The Jackson are over _____, washing_____car.

your/you're: 13. _____ going to drop _____ ice cream!

colonel/kernel: 14. _____ Chavez eats his popcorn one _____ at a time.

banned/band: 15. Our _____ was _____ from the fair because we're too loud.

weight/wait: 16. _____ for help before trying to lift that much _____.

sense/cents: 17. If Jolene had any _____, she'd have saved more than fifty

_____ by now.

Spell Check

READ each sentence. CIRCLE the homophone that's wrong. Then WRITE the RIGHT homophone in the blank.

Example: We burn would in our fireplace. _wood_

1. Toby choose gum all the time! _____

2. Too bad they band chewing gum at school. _____

3. Have you ever traveled oversees? _____

4. Uncle Jim climbed Mount Kisco's highest peek. _____

5. Simka's mom is a kernel in the army. _____

6. Who would ever want to be a school principle? _____

7. I bet you can't lift that heavy wait! _____

8. Don't waist so much paper! Use both sides. _____

9. That pot is two hot to touch! Use an oven mitt. _____

10. I want to travel all over the whirled. _____

11. Be my guessed! _____

12. Wearing a bike helmet is common cents. _____

13. People always prays my mom's apple pie. _____

14. If you take an aspirin, it will lesson the pain. _____

15. The Rubins called. There not coming over tonight. _____

16. I'm feeling some gilt about not helping set the table. _____

Spotlight on Homographs

Some words are spelled the same but sound different (the opposite of homophones!). These are called HOMOGRAPHS. Sometimes, changing the vowel sound gives a word a different meaning. You already know how to spell these words, so don't be confused by the way they sound!

DRAW a line to connect each word on the left with the correct meaning on the right.

Multiple Meaning Word
Example: read (rhymes with red)

Definition
past tense of to read

1. dove (rhymes with love) ____
2. dove (rhymes with stove) ____
3. bow (rhymes with now) ____
4. bow (rhymes with snow) ____
5. wind (rhymes with pinned) ____
6. wind (rhymes with kind) ____
7. lead (rhymes with red) ____
8. lead (rhymes with feed) ____
9. tear (rhymes with stare) ____
10. tear (rhymes with steer) ____
11. bass (rhymes with space) ____
12. bass (rhymes with pass) ____
13. sow (rhymes with now) ____
14. sow (rhymes with snow) ____
15. live (rhymes with give) ____
16. live (rhymes with drive) ____

a. hair ribbon
b. low musical sound or guitar
c. to twist and turn
d. to plant seeds
e. a kind of fish
f. gusty breeze
g. to breathe, exist
h. not dead
i. a kind of bird
j. to go in front, take charge
k. past tense of *to dive*
l. to rip
m. kind of metal or past tense verb *to lead*
n. drop that comes from your eyes
o. to bend over
p. mama pig

Keywords

The harder the word, the harder the homophone. Once you get a handle on these words, you'll be a super speller!

READ the paragraph. The words in **bold** are your keywords.

> Vincent won't **loan** me ten bucks to go to the carnival at the **naval** air base, even though he's the **heir** to some giant fortune. I guess cheapness is in his **genes**, because his dad's that way too. And now I'm **mourning** the fact that I have to get new **jeans** because I ripped mine this **morning** trying to climb the carnival fence. Well, that effort was totally in **vain**, plus I got a cut just above my **navel**, which is bleeding like crazy. It must've hit a **vein**. Mom says even though I'm the **lone** kid in the house, I make enough trouble for ten. Whatever!

FILL IN the blanks with the **bold** words in alphabetical order.

1. _____
2. _____
3. _____
4. _____
5. _____
6. _____
7. _____
8. _____
9. _____
10. _____
11. _____
12. _____

Blank Out!

FILL IN the blanks with the correct keyword to finish the sentence.

1. No one else could go to the party, so I was the

   _____ guest.

2. Cassie wears her favorite _____ twice a week.

3. The _____ to the king will someday get the crown.

4. My sister's _____ is an "outtie," but mine's an "innie."

5. Honoria is so pale, you can see every _____ in her neck.

6. Mrs. Stein is still in _____ for Elvis, even though he died

   like a million years ago!

7. Dad took us to see the ships at the _____ museum.

8. Lila thinks she'll live to be a

   hundred, because she's got good _____.

9. Luke dove to the ground in a _____ attempt to catch the

   ball. He failed.

10. Hey, would you _____ me five bucks? I'm good for it!

Check It!

Page 107

Spell Check

1. mantel	9. core
2. effect	10. navel
3. edition	11. genes
4. except	12. lightening
5. weighs	13. affect
6. prey	14. principles
7. bred	15. profit
8. boulder	16. ceiling

Page 108
Spotlight

1. CONduct, conDUCT
2. CONflict, conFLICT
3. CONtent, conTENT
4. CONtest, conTEST
5. reCORD, REcord
6. obJECT, OBject
7. proTEST, PROtest
8. reFUSE, REFuse

1. CONtest, conTEST
2. conDUCT, CONduct
3. CONtent, conTENT
4. obJECT, OBject

Word Blocks

FILL IN the word blocks with words of the same shape to finish the homophone pair.

Example:

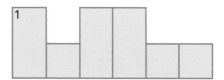

1

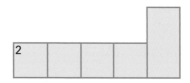

2

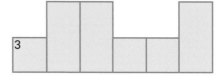

3

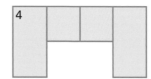

4

5

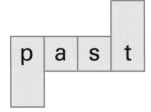

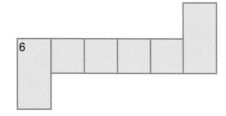

6

Blank Out!

FILL IN the blanks with the right homophones.

utter
udder

1. Anna touched the cow's

_____ with a look of _____ disgust.

ceiling
sealing

2. The handyman is _____ all the cracks in

our _____.

foreword
forward

3. In the book's _____, the author looks

_____ to the future.

prey
pray

4. Let's _____ that that big hawk doesn't think of us

as _____.

stationary
stationery

5. While the train is _____, I'll write a letter on my

new _____.

lightening
lightning

6. Bolts of _____ were _____ the sky in

flashes.

past
passed

7. My fight with Judi is in the _____. A lot of time

has _____ since then.

vein
vain

8. My mom is very _____, and she hates that

_____ sticking out of her forehead.

Spell Check

READ each sentence. CIRCLE the homophone that's wrong. Then WRITE the RIGHT homophone in the blank.

1. Mom loves that ugly clock on the fireplace mantle. _____

2. The cold weather doesn't have any affect on me. _____

3. I can't wait to get the next addition of *Comics Monthly*! _____

4. Katrina is a nice girl, accept she talks a lot. _____

5. I bet my brain ways 300 pounds! _____

6. Kitty Fluff-Fluff is stalking her pray. _____

7. Pugs were bread to be lap dogs. Aren't they cute? _____

8. Watch out! That big bolder is about to fall off the cliff! _____

9. Don't leave that apple corps on the table! _____

10. Gina drew a face on her belly and her naval was the nose. _____

11. I inherited my dad's jeans, which gave me blue eyes. _____

12. Luis is lightning up his room with yellow paint. _____

13. If we lose this game, it will effect our standings. _____

14. Kirby is trying to teach me the basic principals of chess. _____

15. We made a big prophet from our band candy sale. _____

16. Eek! There's a giant spider on the sealing! _____

Spotlight on Stressing Out with Homographs

You know how to STRESS a syllable, right? It means you say it louder. Some homographs sound different because of the syllable that gets stressed, but these words are still spelled same way. For example, DESert vs. deSERT.

READ the words twice, putting the stress first on one syllable, then the other.

	Stress First Syllable	**Stress Second Syllable**
1. conduct	behavior	to lead
2. conflict	a war or battle	to disagree or clash
3. content	information or insides	happy
4. contest	a game or match	to disagree or fight against
5. record	a saved sound or event	to save a sound or event
6. object	a thing	be against something
7. protest	a public complaint	to voice a complaint
8. refuse	garbage	to say no

Most of the time, stressing the first syllable means a noun, and stressing the second syllable means a verb. CIRCLE the stressed syllable for each **bold** word.

1. Khaled won the **contest**, but Ricky will **contest** the results.

2. You **conduct** the band well, but your personal **conduct** is very bad.

3. That game site has so much **content**! It'll keep me **content** for a while.

4. You can hardly **object** to such a harmless **object**.

Keywords

Time to level up! If you want to be a true spelling master, you need to learn some tough words.

READ the paragraph. The words in **bold** are your keywords.

I have zero **experience** with fame, but I know that **publicity** is very important. I mean, actors love to be recognized by **enthusiastic** fans. And some people do **mischievous** things just to get their names in the paper. But others work hard to keep everyone **ignorant** of their **identity**. Like, in order to **detect** spies or gather **intelligence**, secret agents need to **preserve** their "cover." They have to **behave** as normally as possible, so they don't attract **suspicion**. As for me, I'm going into **politics**, so I need all the publicity I can get!

FILL IN the blanks with the **bold** words in alphabetical order.

1. _____
2. _____
3. _____
4. _____
5. _____
6. _____

7. _____
8. _____
9. _____
10. _____
11. _____
12. _____

✓ Check It!

Page 109
Keywords

1. behave
2. detect
3. enthusiastic
4. experience
5. identity
6. ignorant
7. intelligence
8. mischievous
9. politics
10. preserve
11. publicity
12. suspicion

Page 110
Morph It!

1. behavior, behavioral
2. detectably
3. enthusiasm, enthusiastic
4. experience
5. identity, identifiably
6. ignorance, ignorant
7. intelligence, intelligently
8. mischievous, mischievously
9. politics, political
10. preservation
11. publicity, publicly
12. suspicious, suspiciously

Page 111
Criss Cross

Across	Down
1. enthusiasm	1. experience
4. intelligent	2. identity
5. behavior	3. mischievous
7. publicize	4 ignorance

Page 112
Spell Check

1. suspicion
2. identify
3. political
4. behavioral
5. publicly
6. detective
7. enthusiastically
8. mischief
9. preservation
10. ignorance
11. intelligently
12. undetectable
13. inexperienced
14. politicize
15. unidentifiable
16. misbehaved

 Check It!

Page 113

Spotlight

1. but•ton•hole
2. care•tak•er
3. eye•glass•es
4. bod•y•guard
5. girl•friend
6. ev•er•green
7. fin•ger•nail
8. fresh•wa•ter
9. hand•ker•chief
10. high•way
11. jel•ly•bean
12. hu•man•kind
13. pep•per•mint
14. pine•ap•ple
15. show•room
16. ta•ble•spoon

Page 114

Author! Author!

Check to be sure you used six of the words. Then look them up in a dictionary to see if you used them correctly.

Morph It!

FILL IN the blanks by writing the correct form of the word.

	Noun	Adjective	Adverb
1.			behaviorally
2.	detective	detectable	
3.			enthusiastically
4.		experienced	
5.		identifiable	
6.			ignorantly
7.		intelligent	
8.	mischief		
9.			politically
10.		preservative	
11.		public	
12.	suspicion		

Criss Cross

FILL IN the grid by answering the clues with versions of keywords.

ACROSS

1. Excitement, energy, delight

4. Smart

5. The way you act (good or bad)

7. To make public

DOWN

1. If you've done it before, you've got___.

2. Your name and other information about you

3. Wicked, annoying, or bad

4. State of being uninformed

Word Challenge

Spell Check

READ each sentence. CIRCLE the word that's wrong. Then FILL IN the blanks with the correct words. Spell them right!

1. I have a strong suspectment that I'm getting an MP3 player. _____

2. Investigators can identize a corpse by its teeth. _____

3. This country has two main politicious parties. _____

4. My little brother has behavement problems. _____

5. The star publically denied the rumor about losing his dog. _____

6. Sherlock Holmes is my favorite detector. He's a genius! _____

7. My dog Pepper always greets me enthusiastially. _____

8. October 30th is mischievement night in our town. _____

9. The preservement of old movies is so important. _____

10. Will you live your whole life in ignorification of inequality? _____

11. My Dad always explains things very intelligencely. _____

12. There was a nearly undetectifiable smell of wet dog. _____

13. I'm too inexperiencious to ski down a steep mountain. _____

14. The newspapers tried to politify the mayor's wedding. _____

15. With his new beard and glasses, Mr. Hinks is unidentical. _____

16. I'm dead tired. The girl I baby-sit misbehaviored all day! _____

Spotlight on Compound Words

As you already know, a compound word is a word made by sticking two words together. As the words get harder to spell, so do the compounds. Let's pound a few together and see!

MATCH a word on the left with one on the right to make a compound. DRAW a line to connect the two words. FILL IN the blanks with the compound words you matched.

SPLIT the words into syllables, using dots to mark the breaks.

Example: cow   boy   cow•boy

1.	button	friend	_____
2.	care	water	_____
3.	eye	room	_____
4.	body	way	_____
5.	girl	mint	_____
6.	ever	kind	_____
7.	finger	guard	_____
8.	fresh	kerchief	_____
9.	hand	green	_____
10.	high	spoon	_____
11.	jelly	apple	_____
12.	human	hole	_____
13.	pepper	taker	_____
14.	pine	bean	_____
15.	show	glasses	_____
16.	table	nail	_____

Author! Author!

It's your turn to do the writing. Use at least six of the words to write a story, a poem, or a list of crazy sentences. Have fun!

banned	bass	contest	guilty
lightning	medal	mischief	navel
overdue	praise	suspicious	verse

Stack Up

SORT the words into the categories.

accept	adventure	behavioral	bodyguard
colonel	energetic	except	handkerchief
inventor	kernel	permissive	prevention

"Ven" Root
Example: convene

1. _____
2. _____
3. _____

Adjectives
Example: suspicious

1. _____
2. _____
3. _____

Homophones
Example: past/passed

1. _____ / _____
2. _____ / _____

Compound Words
Example: jellybean

1. _____
2. _____

✓ Check It!

Page 115
Stack Up

"Ven" Root
1. adventure
2. inventor
3. prevention

Adjectives
1. behavioral
2. energetic
3. permissive

Homophones
1. accept / except
2. colonel / kernel

Compound Words
1. bodyguard
2. handkerchief

Page 116
Blank Out!

1. corpse
2. convert
3. capitol
4. submit
5. reproduce
6. manage
7. diverse
8. predict
9. adventurous
10. finish
11. equinox
12. captive
13. manipulate
14. convenient
15. conduct
16. admit
17. infinite
18. equality

Page 117
Word Blocks

1. mantel
2. corps
3. heir
4. mourning
5. traitor
6. prophet

Page 118
Morph It!

1. disagreement, disagree, disagreeable
2. apologize, apologetic, apologetically
3. civilization, civilize, civilly
4. competition, competitive, competitively
5. confusion, confusingly
6. contradiction, contradictory, contradictorily
7. decision, decisive, decisively
8. definition, definite, definitely
9. description, descriptive
10. energize, energetic, energetically

Blank Out!

FILL IN the blanks with the correct roots. You can use the roots more than once.

fin	mit	ven	dic/dict	duc/duct
man	corp	cap	equi/equa	vert/vers

1. A dead body   ___ ___ ___ ___se

2. To change into something else   con___ ___ ___ ___

3. Where the government hangs out   ___ ___ ___itol

4. To give in   sub___ ___ ___

5. Make a copy   repro___ ___ ___e

6. To take things into your own hands   ___ ___ ___age

7. Different, varied, multicultural   di___ ___ ___ ___e

8. To say or guess something beforehand   pre___ ___ ___ ___

9. Very exciting, possibly dangerous   ad___ ___ ___turous

10. To end something   ___ ___ ___ish

11. When day and night are the same length   ___ ___ ___ ___nox

12. Someone who has been taken   ___ ___ ___tive

13. To control someone   ___ ___ ___ipulate

14. Easy, not a hassle at all   con___ ___ ___ient

15. To lead, like a band   con___ ___ ___ ___

16. To let someone in, or to confess   ad___ ___ ___

17. With no ending   in___ ___ ___ite

18. When everyone is treated the same   ___ ___ ___ ___lity

Word Blocks

FILL IN the word blocks with words of the same shape to finish the homophone pair.

Example:

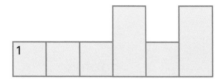

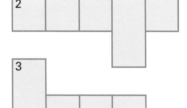

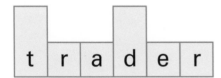

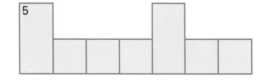

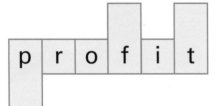

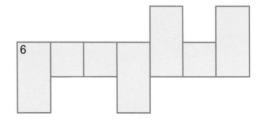

Morph It!

FILL IN the blanks by writing the correct form of the word.

	Noun	Verb	Adjective	Adverb
1.				disagreeably
2.	apology			
3.			civil	
4.		compete		
5.		confuse	confusing	
6.		contradict		
7.		decide		
8.		define		
9.		describe		descriptively
10.	energy			

Spelling Words Index